Ernest Dowson

By THOMAS BURNETT SWANN

Twayne Publishers, Inc. :: New York

To: *My Father, with Admiration and Love*

Preface

Though some critics insist that a poet should be read for his work and not for his life, it is hard to read *Don Juan* without identifying the romantic hero with "bad, mad" Lord Byron, or *Sonnets from the Portuguese* without remembering that the author was rescued from invalidism and a tyrannical father by the knight errantry of Robert Browning. Indeed, so long as the poet is intrinsically good, there is justification for reading his poems in the light of his life. Ernest Dowson is such a poet, and his work gains additional magic from the tragedy of his unrequited love for Adelaide Foltinowicz and his early death from consumption. It is the purpose of this study to examine the work for its own merit but not to divorce it from Dowson's life or from the legend he lived even before he died; to show how his poems, sketches, stories, and novels came to be written; how they celebrate and sometimes reproach the girl who did not return his love; how they anticipate and sometimes entreat the death which soon but too slowly released him.[1]

With Dowson there is little problem of obscurity and little need for detailed interpretations. He is not like Eliot, who had to footnote his own *Waste Land,* nor like e. e. cummings, who punctuated according to whim instead of rule. Nor is there the task of evaluating a large body of critical opinion about Dowson. He has not been a popular subject with writers of dissertations and scholarly articles, and most of the writings about him, reflecting the vigor of his legend, are reminiscent rather than critical. The problem then is largely a matter of tracing the common themes which unite his work, of evaluating particular poems, and of relating them to his fellow writers of the Decadence or to the Latin authors Horace and Propertius from whom he borrowed. As with most lyric poets, criticism must yield now and then to simple appreciation; when poems become perfect song, detailed analysis is a desecration.

With some poets the best approach is chronological, a study of their growth and development from year to year, decade to decade. Dowson is not such a poet. In the first place he died young and his career was limited to little more than the 1890's; in the second place, he failed to develop even in the 1890's. His second book of poems, *Decorations,* published in 1899, is hardly distinguishable from his *Verses* of 1896. Once he had reached poetic maturity in his early twenties, his poems neither introduced new subjects nor treated old ones in new ways. It was the same with his stories and novels. If anything, there was a slight lessening in power, though never in polish; an increasing dependence on his models, Swinburne, Verlaine, and Henry James. A useful approach, then, after an introductory chapter to place him in his period, is to start with his best work, the poems, and to group them by subject in the following two chapters: "For Love of Adelaide" (poems about love) and "The Hollow Land" (poems about nature, death, religion, and escape); and then to divide the chapters into smaller divisions, "Child Love," "Lost Love," etc. These divisions must sometimes be arbitrary, since a poem may concern lost love as well as child love, religion as well as death; they are made for convenience and not to rigidly categorize. It is pointless to analyze every poem in detail; there are too many repetitions of subject and mood. The few omitted, or mentioned but not discussed, are those which resemble better or more characteristic poems that have already been treated. The chapter on his verse play, *The Pierrot of the Minute,* properly follows the two chapters on his poems; then comes a chapter on his fourteen stories and sketches (published in *Decorations,* in *Dilemmas,* and in such magazines as *The Savoy* and *The Yellow Book*) and on his translations from the French; a chapter on his two novels written in collaboration with Arthur Moore, *A Comedy of Masks* and *Adrian Rome;* and, finally, a concluding chapter to summarize his achievement.

The wife of Dowson's benefactor, Robert Sherard, remarked in her old age, "I have known great poets: Ernest Dowson died in my arms." [2] To call him a great poet is to burden him with obligations his work cannot fulfill. Greatness implies not only the consummate craftsmanship he did possess, but also a range and variety far beyond his grasp. He is, however, a minor poet of the first rank—first among the second, as Dylan Thomas might have said. His legend, though glamorous, may one day begin to fade along with that of the 1890's, the decade of artful sighs and elegant sins. But his poems, enriched by the legend yet strong in their own right, promise to endure as monuments not to an era nor even to a girl named Adelaide, but to the poet who carved his words like ivory.

THOMAS BURNETT SWANN

Acknowledgments

I wish to acknowledge with gratitude a large debt to Mark Longaker, Professor of English at the University of Pennsylvania, whose definitive biography of Dowson has supplied me with many biographical details, as well as with inspiration, and whose annotated editions of Dowson's poems and stories have been my main primary sources. I am also grateful to Marcia Stille, Professor of Latin at Florida Southern College, who helped me to understand the poet's indebtedness to Horace and Propertius, and who helped me to translate some of his Latin titles into English. Finally, I am indebted to Guy Harrison's bibliography of Dowson in Victor Plarr's *Ernest Dowson* (1914).

Thanks are due also to the following publishers: G. P. Putnam for permission to quote from Bernard Muddiman's *The Men of the Nineties,* copyright 1921. The University of Pennsylvania Press for permission to quote from Mark Longaker's *Ernest Dowson,* copyright 1944; *The Stories of Ernest Dowson,* edited by Mark Longaker, copyright 1947; *The Poems of Ernest Dowson,* edited by Mark Longaker, copyright 1962. Houghton Mifflin Company and Twayne Publishers for permission to quote from Amy Lowell's "Lilacs" in *A Shard of Silence,* copyright 1957. The Citadel Press for permission to quote from *Baudelaire, Rimbaud, Verlaine: Selected Verse and Prose Poems,* edited by Joseph M. Bernstein, copyright 1947.

Contents

Chronology

1867   Ernest Dowson, born August 2 in Lee, Kent, England, the first of two sons, to Alfred Dowson, a sometime littérateur who owned Bridge Dock in Limehouse.

1873   Visits the French Riviera with his family, on one of many attempts to find a climate favorable to his father's consumption.

1886   Matriculates at Queen's College, Oxford; "Sonnet—To a Little Girl," his first published poem, appears in *London Society*.

1887   Meets Lionel Johnson at Oxford and begins a lifelong friendship.

1888   "Souvenirs of an Egotist," his first published story, appears in *Temple Bar;* leaves Oxford without a degree to work sporadically at his father's dock, to further his literary career, and to join a club of merrymakers called "The Bingers."

1890   Acts as assistant editor and contributor to the short-lived magazine, *The Critic*.

1891   Converted to Catholicism; meets Adelaide Foltinowicz, the twelve-year-old daughter of a Polish restaurant owner; "Cynara," his most famous poem, published in *The Century Guild Hobby Horse*.

1891   Becomes active in the Rhymers' Club.

1892   Begins work on *A Comedy of Masks* in collaboration with Arthur Moore.

1893   Proposes marriage to Adelaide, who rejects him with a reminder of her extreme youth but offers the hope that she may change her mind.

1893–   Increases his dependence on alcohol and forms a liaison
1894   with a courtesan named Dulcie.

1894 Translates Zola's *La Terre* for the Lutetian Society; suffers symptoms of increasing severity and realizes that he has contracted the same disease which afflicts his parents; his father dies from an overdose of chloral and a few months later his mother hangs herself; his brother Rowland departs to become a rancher in Canada.

1895 Meets Leonard Smithers, who becomes his publisher and patron; risks public scorn by attending the trial of Oscar Wilde to show his sympathy; tours Flanders and Brittany with the novelist Conal O'Riordan, who the following year dedicates *A Fool and His Heart* to him.

1896 Mourns in France at the funeral of Verlaine, one of his literary idols; contributes poems and stories to *The Savoy,* the new magazine published by Leonard Smithers, edited by Arthur Symons, and illustrated by Aubrey Beardsley.

1896 Dedicates *Verses,* his first collection of poems, to Adelaide; meets the novelist Gertrude Atherton at Pont-Aven in France, where she tries with momentary success to reform him.

1897 Learns that Adelaide is to marry her father's waiter and cries "for madder music and for stronger wine"; *The Pierrot of the Minute* published in a small but exquisite edition with illustrations by Beardsley; befriends Wilde after his release from prison but parts company with him over the matter of a loan.

1899 Wanders about Paris, penniless and alone; discovered by Robert Sherard in a small cafe and given temporary shelter; returns to England late in the year, his health broken by ill health, poverty, and absinthe.

1900 February 23, dies in Sherard's London apartment while making plans for the books he still hopes to write.

1937 His unkept grave discovered in Lewisham Cemetery, London, and visited by five admirers, one of them his old friend Edgar Jepson.

CHAPTER 1

The Decadence

ERNEST DOWSON is usually identified with the Decadents, a group of poets, novelists, and artists who flourished in England during the 1890's and in France during the
entire second half of the nineteenth century. It is wrong to
flatly categorize him as a Decadent and then dismiss him. But
it is also wrong to treat him in a vacuum, apart from the
movement in which he shared and which he helped to shape.
"Decadence" as a term is sometimes equated with "Aestheticism," but more accurately the Decadence is the final phase,
not the whole, of Aestheticism. While Dowson is sometimes
called an Aesthete instead of a Decadent, the second term—the
term to be used in this study—is much more descriptive of his
art, with its air of decay and finality and its morbid concern
with death.

I History

Aestheticism, the parent of Decadence, was in Gautier's
phrase the pursuit of "art for art's sake," the creation and the
appreciation of beauty unburdened with messages and morals.
Beauty to the Aesthetes included an element of strangeness,
a love for the far away: for eras remote in history and islands
remote in miles; for legendary temptresses, Helen and Circe
and Guinevere, and for heroic lovers, Ulysses and Oisen and
Lancelot. "Who dreamed that beauty passes like a dream?"
sang Yeats, an Aesthete who became a Decadent; and poets
wooed beauty in poems, painters in pictures. The act of living,
no less than writing or painting, came to be regarded as an
art, and one which required the same discrimination that the
poet lavished on his words and the painter on his oils and

charcoals. Yeats summarizes the history of Aestheticism in his short story, "Rosa Alchemica": "I remembered, as I read, that mood which Edgar Poe found in a wine-cup, and how it passed into France and took possession of Baudelaire, and from Baudelaire passed to England and the Pre-Raphaelites, and then again to France, and still wanders the world, enlarging its power as it goes, awaiting the time when it shall be, perhaps, alone, or, with other moods, master over a great new religion, and an awakener of the fanatical wars that hovered in the gray surges, and forget the wine-cup where it was born." [1]

He might have added, had he been writing a history instead of a short story, that the mood came to Poe not only from the wine cup but from the English Romantics—Coleridge, Keats, and DeQuincey. In America, Poe extended and enriched the mood with the incantations of "The Raven" and "Annabel Lee"; in England, Tennyson with "The Lotus Eaters," which early reviewers attacked because it sang but did not preach, and damned with the very word "aestheticism"; and in France, Gautier wrote *Mademoiselle de Maupin*. After them came the Pre-Raphaelites who, sickened by the smoke of factories and the death of forests, sighed for the Middle Ages of their imagination. Dante Gabriel Rossetti wove the dark wizardry of "Sister Helen" and William Morris resurrected Guinevere to speak in her own defense. With John Ruskin to champion them, the Pre-Raphaelites waxed in fame; and their great disciple Swinburne added to Rossetti's sensuousness an alien perversity which he found in Baudelaire's *Flowers of Evil* and in his own turbulent nature. By now Aestheticism was flourishing throughout England and France, but without an official name and without public recognition of its unifying principles. It remained for a shy Oxford don, Walter Pater, to codify the Aesthetic approach to life and to transform a mood into a recognized movement: "Not the fruit of experience but experience itself is the end. A counted number of pulses only is given to us of a variegated, dramatic life. How may we see in them all that is to be seen in them by the finest senses? How shall we pass most swiftly from point to point, and be present always at the focus where the greatest number of vital forces unite in their purest energy? To burn always with this hard, gemlike flame, to maintain this ecstasy, is success in life." [2]

For Pater himself it was enough to maintain ecstasy through writing his marble prose and admiring the art of the Renaissance or of ancient Greece. But the young men at Oxford who heard or read his lectures began to seek experience through less acceptable channels. They flaunted sunflowers in their buttonholes and burned incense in their rooms. They hung their walls with sensual nudes by Simeon Solomon. They grew long hair to affect the look of medieval pages. Their walk became an undulation, their repose a languid abstraction; they looked always as if they were waiting to be sculptured. Such behavior, no doubt, was harmless, if a little ridiculous; but some went further and interpreted the principles of Pater as an excuse for strange experiments in drugs and sex.

One such disciple was Oscar Wilde, a youth more gifted than his master and also bolder. By the time that Wilde had become a young man about London, his mooselike frame incongruously housed in lavender trousers and velvet jacket, Aestheticism was a well-known movement, laughable to some, shocking to others, but irresistible to the young and curious; and Wilde was its best exemplar. Gilbert and Sullivan satirized him as Bunthorne in their comic opera *Patience* (1881), but Wilde was pleased to win notice of any kind, even satirical, and he boldly proceeded to extend his repuation as an elegant sinner with remarks like, "It is better to be beautiful than to be good," and, in the early 1890's, with works like *Salomé* and *The Picture of Dorian Gray*.

By this time Aestheticism, obviously in its final phase, was coming to be called Decadence. The Mauve Decade, the Yellow Nineties, and the Fin de Siècle were different names for the same ten years, the era of the Decadents. Decadence numbered among its adherents the poet and critic Arthur Symons, who was soon to be its historian; Lionel Johnson, who lived a life of monastic chastity but escaped into alcohol and dreams of historical Ireland; William Butler Yeats, with raven locks rioting down his forehead and luminous eyes like those of a young Merlin; Aubrey Beardsley, the *enfant terrible* of the movement, a writer as well as an artist, who became famous at twenty-one and died within five years; and of course Ernest

Dowson, the shyest of all the group but not the least gifted. The men themselves died young, except for Yeats and Symons —Beardsley at twenty-six, Dowson at thirty-three, Johnson at thirty-five, Wilde at forty-four. But the 1890's remain their monument.

Across the Channel, Decadence had properly begun in 1856, when Baudelaire published *The Flowers of Evil,* and it gained impetus in succeeding decades with the absinthe-tinted songs of Verlaine and the inspired ravings of the boy-genius Rimbaud. By the 1890's Verlaine and the late Rimbaud, together with the poet and theorist Stéphane Mallarmé, had come to represent the so-called Symbolist phase of the Decadence, which survived the century and influenced modern poets like Ezra Pound and T. S. Eliot. Preferring suggestion to direct statement, the Symbolists attempted to make poetry aspire toward "the condition of music." They employed symbols to indicate moods, ideas, or objects; and Rimbaud, for example, saw vowels as colors: "A black, E white, I red, U green, O blue. . . ." There were also Decadent novelists. In 1884 Joris Karl Huysmans had written *Against the Grain,* which carried its hero Des Esseintes through every imaginable sensation; and in 1896 Pierre Louÿs rivaled him with *Aphrodite,* a story of ancient Alexandria morbidly colored by nineteenth-century Decadence. Reflecting and sometimes inspiring the poets and the novelists, the painter Gustave Moreau wrought jeweled canvasses—Leda and Salomé, Helen and Galatea—which were praised by Huysmans and Wilde in their novels and mentioned by Dowson in *A Comedy of Masks.*

II *Subject Matter*

The inspiration of the Decadents—though still the exotic beauty which had charmed the Romantics, the young Tennyson, and the Pre-Raphaelites—had changed its habitation. In place of the natural, they prized the artificial; in place of the countryside, the city. The lily, the rose, and the sunflower, it is true, were their symbols and the source of their favorite colors—white, crimson, and gold. But they were hothouse flowers. Though Wilde wore a sunflower in his lapel and carried a lily in his hand, no one ever saw him wielding a hoe in a garden. Deer and meadowlarks, beloved since the time

of Chaucer, fled before the urban cat, "luxurious in perfume."
Ruskin and Morris had preached a return to the countryside
and to the simple values of the past. But even while revering
these men, the Decadents entrenched themselves in the city
and visited the country via the library if at all. The dancehall,
the theater, the bistro; the salon and the boudoir—these were
their favorite haunts. They echoed Baudelaire when he sang
to Paris:

> *Whether thou sleep, with heavy vapours full,*
> *Sodden with day, or, new apparelled, stand*
> *In gold-laced veils of evening beautiful,*
>
> *I love thee, infamous city! Harlots and*
> *Hunted have pleasures of their own to give,*
> *The vulgar herd can never understand.*[3]

The beauty which Keats called truth was altered beyond
recognition; she was rather like a country lass who had gone
to the city, lost her becoming plumpness and her apple color-
ing, and affected a French coiffure. She continued to charm
but her charms were of artifice, not nature. On the rare occa-
sions that the Decadents visited the woods, it was usually in
their poems of ancient times, as if they hesitated to face nature
except from a distance. When he wandered the fairy-haunted
forests of Ireland, Yeats invested them with a haze of centuries. But much more often a journey into the past led straight
to the heart of a city. Louÿs conducts us to an Alexandria
which can boast the refined perversions of his own Paris;
Wilde, to a biblical palace where Dorian Gray would have felt
at home.

The vices one finds in the Decadents, in the men as well as
their works, are predictably those of advanced civilization and
of sophisticated society. When men have machines and ser-
vants to wait on them, to afford leisure and to inflict ennui,
they sometimes find that the old and simple sins have lost
their attraction. Like the surfeited Romans with their orgies
and gladiatorial combats, they demand the perverse and the
strange. Wine is not enough, they must have absinthe; when
absinthe pales, narcotics. Verlaine and Rimbaud, during their
liaison in Paris, intoxicated themselves with both absinthe and

hashish and then wrote poems of hellish and heavenly music. Symons has a poem called "The Opium-Smoker," which may or may not record his own experience; and Dowson in a prose piece, "Absinthia Taetra," celebrates the dissipation which hastened his death.

When the conscience is drugged and the senses sharpened, no sin is beyond the sinning and, later, the recording in a poem or a picture. Baudelaire had pointed the way with *The Flowers of Evil.* In "Lovers of the Damned" his heroines Hippolyta and Delphine seek pleasure together through forbidden embraces; and, though the poet concludes that they are going to hell, he plainly enjoys making the descent with them. Swinburne, an admirer of Baudelaire, follows the same descent in "Anactoria" and *Lesbia Brandon,* and Verlaine, whose love for Rimbaud had taught him abnormal psychology, in "Young Girls at School." Male homosexuality, of course, is the secret vice of Dorian Gray, implied if not explicit. There is torture too in the Decadents, a fascination for pain inflicted on or by beautiful women and boys: the masochistic hero of Louÿs' *The Woman and the Puppet,* who encourages his mistress to beat him with a whip; the ghastly and senseless crucifixion of the slave girl in *Aphrodite;* the decapitated head of John the Baptist, painted by Gustave Moreau and described by Wilde. In the works of the Decadents torture becomes a ritual performed with love and with rapturous brilliance.

Into the making of such perversities went a fierce energy, but one which concealed despair and weariness. The century had begun with promise, and it flowered through its middle decades into rich scientific progress and far-reaching social reforms. But the very effort which had accomplished such advances left many Englishmen weary, and the fact that progress had brought, instead of happiness, increasing spiritual doubt and deep-rooted pessimism left them disillusioned. Hence, gloom and languor pervade the work of the Decadents, who exhale a great, heart-wrenching sigh in the face of ennui, *Weltschmerz,* futility—various names for the same debilitating paralysis. Symons writes a poem called "Satiety" and another in which he sighs with Swinburne, "I have grown tired of sorrow and human tears." The death wish becomes a major theme in Dowson, and his anguished "Cynara" has been called

a "parable of the Decadent soul." In a very real sense the
stylistic perfection—the high and glittering polish of Wilde,
Dowson, and others—is an effort to combat despair. Life is
meaningless, they seem to say. Man is dust in a mindless universe. But at least we can write or paint well; protest our
impermanence through permanent art. In the brilliance of
their best work lies the justification for artificiality, perversion,
and defeatism. Out of these doubtful materials they did indeed
create the enduring poem and the lasting picture.

The achievement of the Decadence, its perverse subject matter redeemed by perfection of form, is well illustrated in a
passage from Beardsley's *Under the Hill,* which describes the
prints on the walls in a bedroom: "Within the delicate curved
frames lived the corrupt and gracious creatures of Dorat and
his school, slender children in masque and domino smiling
horribly, exquisite lechers leaning over the shoulders of smooth
doll-like girls and doing nothing in particular, terrible little
Pierrots posing as lady lovers and pointing at something outside the picture, and unearthly fops and huge birdlike women
mingling in some rococo room, lighted mysteriously by the
flicker of a dying fire that throws great shadows upon wall
and ceiling." [4] Here is the artificiality of a decaying society,
with its fops and masks and rococo rooms. Here is perversion,
implied by such adjectives as "corrupt," "terrible," "unearthly";
by the lecher and the "terrible little Pierrots posing as lady
lovers." Here is fatigue: the lechers are leering but "doing
nothing in particular," and the fire is dying. But the passage is
unforgettable, a single long sentence sustained with rococo
grace and with eerie images which linger in the mind. Like
the frantically lighthearted dancers in "The Masque of the
Red Death," the creatures of Beardsley are caught by the
marble of words in the midst of their leering folly.

III *Publications*

The Decadents praised and criticized each other's poetry,
but they were human enough to seek a wider audience; and
the reading public, deliciously shocked by writers who would
have caused Wordsworth to blush and Mrs. Browning to
swoon, stood ready to buy if not to approve of their works.
Three publishers specialized in Decadent books—Elkin Ma-

thews, John Lane, and especially Leonard Smithers, who paid to Dowson the small but regular fee of thirty shillings a week for his translations, and who published "The Ballad of Reading Gaol" after Wilde's imprisonment when there was every reason to believe that the poem would find no audience. To illustrate their books, these publishers engaged the precocious Beardsley, who seemed, with his attenuated, consumption-ravaged body and his metallic red hair, to illustrate one of his own drawings. Printed perhaps on Japanese vellum and bound in the richest cloth, Decadent books showed consummate craftsmanship. It is true that Lane and Mathews, then partners, gave Dowson's *Dilemmas* an inferior binding, but his *Pierrot of the Minute* became, in the hands of Smithers, a little gem of bookmaking, with Beardsley drawings to adorn the cover and text. Even the Decadent magazines, *The Yellow Book* and *The Savoy*, were bound in hard covers and illustrated by men of genius.

The Yellow Book, published during the years between 1894 and 1897, excelled in content as well as in format. Though conservative writers like Henry James and Edmund Gosse contributed to several issues, the prevailing tone was Decadent; and the public's reaction was one of shocked curiosity. No one today, in this era of *Playboy* and *Eros*, could take offense at the magazine; but the late Victorians—accustomed to stories and poems which made a point, protested poverty, or preached compassion—were shocked by the lack of message. *The Yellow Book* frankly served "art for art's sake," not morality's. Worse, the colors were brash, and the drawings by Beardsley whispered and sometimes shouted sexual license. He painted with elegant eroticism: sly hermaphrodites, knowing infants, and ladies whose look was an invitation. Also, the magazine was bound like a book, as if it presumed to claim permanence for its then obscure young contributors, Richard LeGallienne, Max Beerbohm, Symons, Yeats, and Dowson.

After the trial of Oscar Wilde in 1895, Beardsley was mistakenly linked with him in perversion and dropped from the magazine, which began a rapid decline. In 1896 the publisher Smithers decided to found a rival and, he hoped, successor to the dying *Yellow Book*. He engaged Symons as editor and summoned Beardsley from seclusion to become his illustrator.

Together they launched *The Savoy,* whose daring matched its excellence. The second issue is typical. Not even Victorians, it is true, could protest the sentimental verse playlet, "The Love of the Poor," and Dowson's entries are equally harmless. His poem "Saint Germain-en-Laye" is a seasonal poem rather than a poem of sin like "Cynara," and his story "Countess Marie of the Angels" is as innocuous as its title. But the Decadent spirit is elsewhere strong. Vincent O'Sullivan's article, "On the Kind of Fiction Called Morbid," defends an important aspect of Decadence: its concern with decay and death. Yeats' philosophical story, "Rosa Alchemica," in spite of a moral conclusion, revels in paganism; and Symons, the editor, includes a story of his own in which a fallen woman, far from being punished, begins a career which promises to prove both profitable and pleasurable. Furthermore, the people depicted in lithographs by Charles Shannon are nude, and the drawings by Beardsley have that air of secret and enjoyed depravity for which he had become notorious in *The Yellow Book.* Beardsley is also represented by a selection from his novel, *Under the Hill,* a phallic version of the Venus and Tannhäuser legend.

The British public, which had bought the first issues of *The Yellow Book* even while professing shock, rejected its rival from the start. The trials and imprisonment of Wilde were fresh in their minds, and Beardsley's name had not been cleared of the whispers which linked him with the same or similar scandals. It was even rumored—and this time with truth—that Beardsley had drawn a sexually aroused bull for the cover of the first *Savoy* and with great difficulty been persuaded to substitute a harmless garden scene. The magazine was doomed. As Yeats wrote:

We might have survived but for our association with Beardsley; perhaps, for his *Under the Hill,* a Rabelaisian fragment promising a literary genius as great as his artistic genius; and for the refusal of the bookseller who controlled the railway bookstalls to display our wares. The bookseller's manager, no doubt looking for a design of Beardsley's, pitched upon Blake's "Anteus setting Vergil and Dante upon the verge of Cocytus" as the ground of refusal, and when Arthur Symons pointed out that Blake was considered a "very spiritual artist," replied, "O, Mr. Symons, you must remember that we have an audience of young ladies as well as an audience of agnostics." [5]

In a single year the "audience of young ladies," or those who passed as their guardians, managed to extinguish the boldest and most brilliant magazine of the decade. To *The Yellow Book* Dowson had contributed a single story, "Apple Blossom in Brittany"; to *The Savoy*, which had been his principal outlet, he had sent both poems and stories. The magazine's extinction depressed his spirits and reduced his meager circumstances. He was not aware, however, that more than a magazine had suffered; Decadence itself, shaken by the fall of Wilde, had received a shock from which it never recovered. Through the next four years, the movement which had glorified death quietly sickened and died.

IV *Dowson and the Decadents*

Most of the English Decadents were friends or acquaintances of Dowson. He joined Symons, LeGallienne, Yeats, Johnson, and others in the Rhymers' Club, a loosely organized group of poets who met in the Cheshire Cheese where, ensconced with beer mugs and churchwarden pipes, they recited their poetry and exchanged comments. By no means all of the Rhymers were Decadents, but Pater, Swinburne, Rossetti, and Verlaine were the literary idols of the group. Moreover, the two Rhymers' Club anthologies—which included such titles as "Night," "Lost," and "Euthanasia (Fin de Siècle)," as well as Dowson's "Cynara"—abounded in Decadent themes. Dowson's association with the Rhymers extended beyond the meetings. Symons was later to become the editor of *The Savoy*, which published Dowson's poems and stories. LeGallienne, a onetime reader for Mathews and Lane, helped to win acceptance for Dowson's manuscript, *Dilemmas*. Lionel Johnson remained Dowson's friend for life, and they often talked away the night to escape the insomnia which troubled Dowson and tormented Johnson.

Some of Dowson's Decadent friends were not in the Rhymers' Club. He knew Oscar Wilde before his arrest, stood by him during the trial, and visited him in France after Wilde's release from prison. Eventually the men quarreled because of a loan from Wilde which Dowson was slow to repay. Later reconciled, they remained on good terms until their deaths in the same year, 1900. Another friend—so Dowson thought— was the artist Beardsley, who illustrated his *Pierrot of the Minute* and whose sister performed the role of the moon maiden when the play was produced in London. Beardsley secretly disliked Dowson; he thought his play dull and the man himself disreputable. But the gentle-hearted Dowson did not know Beardsley's opinion or knew and did not take offense. He visited Beardsley on his deathbed and attended his Requiem Mass at the Farm Street Church. His acquaintance with Decadents extended to Frenchmen as well as Englishmen. He went with the Rhymers to hear Verlaine when the famous Symbolist came to lecture in London in 1893 at Barnard's Inn, and after the lecture talked with him at the Constitutional. Later he visited him in Paris and attended his funeral. He also knew Pierre Louÿs and hoped to translate *Aphrodite* into English but lost the commission to another translator even though Louÿs himself had asked for Dowson.

Actual Decadents he knew in large number; their spiritual and literary ancestors he met through books. Poe was one of his idols; he liked his poems but preferred his prose. DeQuincey haunted him with *Confessions of an English Opium-Eater,* and he read Baudelaire—his *Flowers of Evil* as well as his prose poems—with awed admiration. But his favorite was Swinburne. When Dowson was a student at Oxford, the famous poet was living in seclusion with Theodore Watts and his songs of passion had begun to lose their fire. But Dowson admired him as he had been in his youth, singing the loves of a devil with the tongue of an angel. He considered "Dolores" one of the greatest poems in the language, and at Oxford he liked to sit with unkempt hair and wrinkled clothes and discuss "The Garden of Proserpine" with his friends. Poe, DeQuincey, Baudelaire, and Swinburne: tormented geniuses addicted to drugs and alcohol, they were dangerous examples for Dowson the man, but incomparable masters for Dowson the poet.

Both his personal and reading acquaintance with the other Decadents have left their mark on Dowson's work. But resemblances and even evidences of direct influence do not lessen the uniqueness of his achievement. Swinburne, for example, inspired but did not dominate him. The poem which Dowson recited at Oxford, "The Garden of Proserpine," may have prompted his "Villanelle of Acheron," where the same goddess is invoked in the same weary accents. He echoed the subject and phrasing of Swinburne's "A Leave-Taking" in his "Venite Descendamus." Finally, like the greater poet, Dowson employed such difficult verse forms as the rondel, the rondeau, and the villanelle, developed by the French in the Middle Ages and popularized by Charles d'Orleans and François Villon. But there are basic differences. Swinburne is vague and diffuse. He may spin a single thought into several pages of exquisite but repetitive music. He is prodigal with adjectives and addicted to alliteration: "bird of the bitter bright gray golden morn," "somewhere safe to sea." Dowson is much more sparing, and his longest poems are less than two short pages. He treats the same Romantic subjects as Swinburne—lost love, the death wish, pagan goddesses—but with Classical restraint. He is economical without being bare.

Both poets write about sin, but Swinburne far more often and with a more deliberate wish to shock. Dowson may allude to a "bought red mouth" or "Maenad airs," but he never speaks, like Swinburne, of kisses which bruise and bring blood, nor does he revel in the Lesbianism and other perversions which attracted the older poet. Indeed, a hallmark of Dowson's poetry is his love of innocence, his adoration of girlhood and maidenhood. Whatever Adelaide Foltinowicz was in life, she became in his poems a saint and a paragon. Swinburne had no such ideal to inspire and exalt his verses. We remember his ladies of sin—Fustine and Anactaria—and not his virgins.

This same love of innocence separates Dowson from Wilde. He has no poem so frankly sordid as "The Harlot's House," with its "horrible marionettes" and "silhouetted skeletons." His novel *A Comedy of Masks* contains a seduction, but one which is seen in retrospect and not exploited for its power to shock. His villain Lightfoot is hardly a Dorian Gray collecting sins, the more flamboyant the better, as a lepidopterist collects butterflies. Nor does he cultivate a sensual exoticism, as Wilde does in "The Sphinx," for its own effect. Dowson's exoticism is not sensual, and it is not an end in itself but rather a decorative background for his personal and deeply felt sorrow.

What about his fellow Rhymers, Yeats, Johnson, and Symons? Since Dowson met with them to hear and discuss their poems, it is natural to look for echoes in his work, but the differences are far more significant. The Yeats of the 1890's is still a dreamer, lost in the Celtic twilight. He is often deliberately vague. Too much lucidity, he no doubt reasoned, like the sun rising above a marsh, would dissipate his shadows. He wishes the reader to encounter his characters—Oisen and Maeve and Deirdre—as if through a mist which supplies in mystery what is lost in immediacy. Dowson has a twilight of his own, but it is not Celtic, it is more like the Hades of Homer. He may picture a shadowy landscape but his words remain clear; he does not blur them in order to blur his scene. In all of his poetry he is almost never obscure.

Another Rhymer to whom Dowson has been compared is Lionel Johnson. Both men admired the poets of ancient Rome —Horace and others; both found subjects closer at hand in the Catholic Church, to which they came as converts. Their difference is one of quality. With a few exceptions, the poems of Dowson are readable even today. In fact, it is hard for anthologists to choose among them, once they have chosen the inevitable "Cynara." Johnson, however, with the exception of a handful of poems like "The Dark Angel," "To Morfydd," and "By the Statue of King Charles at Charing Cross," has faded like the cover of an old *Yellow Book*. A hint of his crippling weakness appears in the overabundance of exclamation points and "oh's" throughout his volumes, as in the line, "Through glades and glooms! Oh, fair! Oh, sad!" Too often he shouts and postures, as if possessed by the Muse. Perhaps the weakness lay in Johnson, the man. When intoxicated, he loved to hold forth and harangue his friends. Whether his subject was a writer like Thomas Hardy or whether he was lecturing Dowson on the evils of consorting with harlots, he declaimed, he preached, he delivered judgment; and much of his poetry seems written in the same spirit of declamation. Dowson, on the other hand, can relax and lower his voice. Though he feels the sacredness of his profession, he does not attempt to perform like a latter-day Orpheus. He too has his "oh's" and exclamations, but in reasonable number. He sometimes dramatizes but not in excess of the situation.

No more does Dowson resemble that third Rhymer and his onetime editor, Symons. Though Symons attempted most of the subjects popular with the Decadents, among them the death wish prominent in Dowson, he seems always to be playing a role; he writes with competence but without conviction. The pose of the Decadent, a starving one at that, is evident in such a stanza as:

> *I lie on my pallet bed,*
> *And hear the drip of the rain,*
> *The rain on my garret roof is falling,*
> *And I am cold and in pain.*[6]

A great critic and gifted translator, a more than competent editor, Symons failed as a poet in his own right and offers no real comparison with the much superior Dowson. Far from influencing Dowson, he himself was influenced by the better poet, as in his poem "To One in Alienation," which echoes the earlier "Cynara." [7]

Dowson has more in common with Verlaine than with his fellow Rhymers. Four of the poems in *Decorations* are free translations from the Frenchman, and others show his influence. Both poets celebrated the innocence of girlhood and the mysteries of the Catholic Church; both grieved for the passing of beauty, the fading of roses, and the fall of lilies; both divined the tears that lie at the heart of things. But Dowson's difference is in part his difference from Swinburne and Wilde. He lacks Verlaine's diabolism and anger. He has no poems about Lesbians and his Pierrot is not made like Verlaine's for "sensual appetizing" but for "innocent dreaming." In Dowson "breasts upbraid the snow." In Verlaine breasts are "demented." When Verlaine is sad, he is sometimes also cynical, sneering at the evils of the world and the weaknesses in his own soul. Dowson is also sad but with resignation and not with anger.

In spite of resemblances, then, Dowson was more than a Decadent; in one or several aspects he differed from every other member of the group. His differences suggest a further influence, and we have his own admission that he read the

odes of Horace, the love poems of Catullus, and the elegies
of Propertius. The images which had served the Romans—
roses and lilies, wine and moonlight—served him for similar
purposes. He developed a hard clarity which doubtless owes
much to the Latin poets, who, ruthlessly excluding the prolix
and the vague, chiseled their poems as if they were carving
figurines of Carrara marble. He borrowed the names of their
heroines, Cynara, Lalage, and Neobule. He echoed the *carpe
diem* note of Horace. Again and again he caught the pathos of
Propertius' famous lament (*Elegies*, II, 28 A and B):

> *The rhombus sound, a whirl-and-boom beneath the magic song,*
> *Now ceases. The fire has gone out; the laurel is dust.*
> *The moon, unwilling, comes down less often from heaven;*
> *And the bird of darkness utters its sinister warning.*[8]

Of "Cynara" Victor Plarr could justly write: "Horace suggested, but Propertius inspired." [9]

But no good poet is merely the sum of his influences. Dowson has sometimes been called an English Verlaine or an
English Propertius. He is more and less; ultimately, he is himself. Most of his forms and many of his subjects he borrowed.
But what he made of them depended on what he was: a
shy, wistful dreamer, misplaced in his country and his century,
who usually wanted to be somewhere else; who fell in love
with a waitress and idealized her into a saint; who drank too
much absinthe; who, facing starvation, gave his last franc to a
girl of the streets; and who wrote not with anger nor bitterness, but with sorrow sweetened into song. His singing is
neither loud nor insistent, nor is it greatly varied; but it is
unforgettable. The world of his poems is a kind of twilight
or even hell, but the barking of Cerberus is muzzled and the
underground rivers—Styx, Phlegethon, and Acheron—ripple
with melancholy music.

CHAPTER 2

For Love of Adelaide

ERNEST DOWSON was predominantly and incomparably a love poet. He wrote about nature, he wrote about religion and death; but love was his favorite subject, a compulsion as well as a release. More than half of his poems in *Verses* and *Decorations* celebrate or deprecate love and, with a few exceptions, a single girl inspired them: Adelaide Foltinowicz. He did not try to hide the importance of her inspiration. When he dedicated his first book of poems to her, he wrote: "To you, who are my verses. . . ."

Adelaide was the daughter of Polish emigrants who ran a small restaurant, called "Poland," in Soho. She was twelve when Dowson first met her, a waitress in the restaurant, and he was twenty-four. At first he liked her as a child; he admired her artless innocence. Then, undeterred by the difference in their ages, he fell in love. His friends looked askance at Adelaide. Her nose was crooked, her hands were red, she lacked education and poise. But to Dowson her face was charming, even if not beautiful. He praised her accent, which in spite of the neighborhood held no taint of Cockney; and he insisted that her parents had been people of consequence in their native country. For six years he paid her court. During this time she was sometimes cross and sometimes cold, and not always because of her own bad temper. For one thing he annoyed her with his indecisiveness. As he wrote to his friend Sam Smith, "I go on in precisely the same situation in Poland. I can't somehow screw myself up to making a declaration of myself to *Madame*, although I am convinced that it is the most reasonable course." [1] Proscrastination was not his only failing. Sometimes he came to "Poland" intoxicated. "Under the influence of drink," Arthur Symons reports, "he became almost literally insane, certainly quite irresponsible. He fell into furious and unreasoning passions; a vocabulary unknown to him at other times sprang up like a whirlwind; he seemed always about to commit some act of absurd violence." [2] And he might be accompanied by ladies of doubtful reputation who, if Adelaide did not recognize their profession, were all too obvious to her watchful mother. It was no surprise to anyone except Dowson when Adelaide married her father's waiter, Auguste, in 1897. We know little about her life after the marriage. That she bore her husband two children is known; afterward, according to an unauthenticated account, she left him to become a woman of the streets and died from an abortion in the charity ward of a London hospital. Some critics have argued, without real evidence, that she served as the model for Mildred in Somerset Maugham's *Of Human Bondage*.[3] All in all, Adelaide seems to have been a rather ordinary girl who became a very ordinary woman.

Dowson, however, idealized her beyond recognition. After her marriage, Frank Harris said to Dowson:

"You can find a dozen finer gems," I cried, "incomparably more lustrous, more—"
He shrugged his shoulders disdainfully. "More to your taste, I dare say—not to mine." "Can't you see," he burst out with sudden violence, "that I loved her just because you and the others could find nothing in her; no beauty in her curving white neck and the way the dark tendrils curled on it; no sweetness in the pure eyes and mocking gay laughter; nothing. But I saw, and knew she was mine, made for me and me alone to love and possess. . . ." [4]

If there was little for others to see in her, Dowson saw or thought he saw much. She seemed to him just such a maiden as poets enshrine in their poems, his lady and saint, his Stella and Laura. His poems are both lovely and chilling with her presence. Sometimes she is kind, sometimes cold, now a child, now a budding woman, always desirable, ultimately unobtainable; as elusive as an undine. It is true that some of his love poems were not inspired by Adelaide. A few like "Ad Domnulam Suam," "Beyond," "Jadis," and "Libera Me" were written before he met her, and a few others like "The Dead Child" may refer to the daughter of his father's foreman at Bridge Dock. But regardless of their inspiration, they are hardly distinguishable from the poems to Adelaide.

Three of his poems, to be sure, are surprisingly different in mood and in subject matter. They present the poet as a lighthearted lover searching for an easy conquest. In "Soli Cantare Periti Arcades" ("The Arcadians Alone Were Skilled in Singing"), a title he took from Virgil's *Eclogues* 10, 32-33, he imagines himself a shepherd:

> Good luck to you, Paris ladies!
> Ye are over fine and nice,
> I know where the country maid is,
> Who needs not asking twice.[5]

The lines sound Elizabethan. One thinks of Marlowe with his "Passionate Shepherd" and particularly of Thomas Campion, who, following centuries of neglect, was rediscovered in 1889 when A. H. Bullen published a collection of his poems. It is possible that Dowson, before he wrote "Soli . . . ," had read Campion's poem beginning:

> I care not for these ladies,
> That must be wooed and prayed:
> Give me kind Amarillis,
> The wanton country maid.[6]

The poet who rejected the Paris ladies when he spoke as a shepherd returns in "Rondeau" to reconsider their charms. Instead of a country maid, he chooses this time a Gallic gamine named Manon who is saucily housed in a French rondeau:

> Expound, I pray, the mystery
> Why wine-stained lip and languid eye,
> And most unsaintly Maenad air,
> Should move us more than all the rare
> White roses of virginity?
> Ah, Manon, say! (131)

A lighthearted Dowson speaks for the third time in "To His Mistress." This poem begins with a melancholy sigh for the brevity of things but turns Cavalier with the second stanza. In the third stanza Sir John Suckling himself, who once exulted, "Out upon it, I have loved / Three whole days together!" might be addressing his mistress:

> *You ask my love completest,*
> *As strong next year as now,*
> *The devil take you, sweetest,*
> *Ere I make aught such vow.* (117)

All three poems, in their wit and naughtiness, reflect the Elizabethans and the Cavalier poets, who took love where they found it and lingered with Amarillis until they spied Naeara. But the poems can also be read as a covert protest against the virginal rule of Adelaide. Perfection, after all, is demanding company. Just as in life Dowson sometimes drank, caroused, and brought harlots to dine at "Poland," so in three of his poems he frolics with country wenches and city gamines. The frolics are rare but welcome, and more than one reader has confessed the wish that Manon had proved a more frequent rival to Adelaide.

With these exceptions, Dowson's love poems are wistful even in their lightest moments and funereal in their darkest. Because he worships an ideal of inhuman perfection in a world of imperfections, he is faced with a painful and irresolvable conflict. A warm and sensitive man, he humanly yearns for his sweetheart's submission. But if she is flawless, as he believes, how can she lower herself to love him, a human and erring lover? Her yielding would be a confession of weakness, an abasement of her divinity. In spite of his yearning, then, he never allows her a total submission. She may smile and be kind, but she does not yield (or if she yields, it is only for the moment). By various means he contrives to keep her apart from him. Perhaps she is still a child, and there can be no question of physical submission. Perhaps she rejects or ignores him. Perhaps he begs her to seize the day with him but sings in such mournful tones that he runs small risk of acceptance. Sometimes geography separates or threatens to part them, and sometimes, when lesser means seem inadequate, he imagines her dead while he mourns at her grave and half rejoices at her final inaccessibility.

[35]

Readers have sometimes protested the gloom and frustration of Dowson's love poems. Why does he prefer funeral wreaths to bridal bouquets, they ask. Why does he doom his lovers as soon as they begin to love and make them shiver with winter in the flush of spring? At times, such a protest is justified. In his *carpe diem songs*, we shall see, the languor and darkness seem out of place. Much more often, however, the tension of his unresolved conflict—the war between his longing to possess and his fearing that possession means debasement of his ideal— becomes the stuff of fine poetry; it flickers behind his poems like firelight through leaf-thin ivory. Except in "Cynara," he is not a poet of passion, a Byron or an Edna St. Vincent Millay; but rarely have regret and yearning been sung with such haunting persuasiveness.

I *Child Love*

During the reign of Victoria, a curious and attractive phe- nomenon flourished in England: the adoration of girlhood.[7] Lewis Carroll, formal and shy with adults, grew radiant in the company of little girls and wrote his masterpiece, *Alice in Wonderland*, to the small daughter of Henry Liddell, the Classical scholar. At the age of thirty-nine the famous John Ruskin met a nine-year-old child, Rose LaTouche, whom he first admired and then, seven years later, wished to marry. Wisely she declined his proposal, but he loved her until she died. At Oxford during the 1880's little girls enjoyed a remark- able cult among the students, who took them for rides on the river, invited them to tea, and treated them like mascots at athletic events. It is not surprising, then, that girls found their way into literature. Who can forget Little Nell in *The Old Curiosity Shop* or the child Jane Eyre in Charlotte Brontë's novel, or, across the Atlantic, Little Eva in *Uncle Tom's Cabin*? And the child-poems of Swinburne, if not his best, are pleasant and melodious. In contemporary literature the angelic girl is out of fashion; she has yielded in part to the tomboy of Harper Lee's *To Kill a Mockingbird*, in part to the small monster of Lillian Hellman's *The Children's Hour*, a play whose title and theme suggest a new attitude toward childhood—that Long- fellow's innocent hour of storytelling has become an evil hour of taletelling. But Victorian readers liked their little girls immaculate, and Dowson lived in time to share and enrich the tradition.

Dowson came early to his admiration of young girls. Before he was twenty, he had written a sequence of eight poems called "Sonnets of a Little Girl" (one of them became his first published poem in 1886); and in 1890 he contributed an essay called "The Cult of the Child" to a short-lived magazine for which he did editorial work, *The Critic*. After he had met Adelaide Foltinowicz in 1891, the theme of girlhood became pervasive in his poems and stories; and Victor Plarr could write: "It is as an adorer of childhood that his lovers and friends, who have kept his memory green, will best remember him!" [8] Seven of Dowson's poems in *Verses* and *Decorations* treat his love for girlhood and in most of them the inspiration of Adelaide is apparent or probable. She may assume a disguise: as a Breton girl under the grass, as a child in the train of Cupid; but Adelaide, like Cynara, has shed her breath on the poet, and most of his poems reveal her presence. What does he say, through Adelaide, about girlhood? That it is virtuous, shy, wistful, fragile, and charming; and, as such, it must be praised while it endures, preserved as long as possible, and mourned when it dies. To grow is to lose, for maturity offers no real substitute for what it replaces or destroys.

In a pair of comparable poems, "Ad Domnulam Suam" ("To His Little Wife") and "Ad Manus Puellae" ("To the Hands of a Girl"), he celebrates girlhood and intimates that he has no wish for his beloved to pass beyond its boundaries. He wrote the first in 1890, before his acquaintance with Adelaide; but the little waitress is strikingly foreshadowed:

> *Little lady of my heart!*
> *Just a little longer,*
> *Love me: we will pass and part,*
> *Ere this love grow stronger.* (47)

They must love childishly, innocently while they can and then separate before another kind of love can ensnare them. The other kind, the "stronger" love, is much to be avoided. The strengthening of love in this case, one feels, is also a coarsening; gold when mixed with a baser metal becomes stronger but also less pure. In the second poem, which to Dowson's dismay was rejected for inclusion in *The Second Book of the Rhymers' Club*, he sings:

> *I know not the way from your finger-tips,*
> *Nor how I shall gain the higher lands,*
> *The citadel of your sacred lips:*
> *I am captive still of my pleasant bands,*
> *The hands of a girl, and most your hands.* (56)

In actual fact he does not wish to gain the citadel of her sacred lips, the first step toward the "stronger" love of the preceding poem, the physical love which comes inevitably with the years. Captive he remains, and gladly, to his "pleasant bands." Both poems, written with a lightness which belies their ponderous Latin titles, sing rather than speak: the first with the sweet directness of a nursery rhyme, the second with the flourishing elegance of a Cavalier lyric. And both sing the same message: hold to childhood.

But obviously it is impossible to hold always to childhood. Lacking a fountain of youth, we must either grow up or die. In "Yvonne of Brittany," "Villanelle of Sunset," and "The Dead Child," Dowson dooms his sweethearts to an early death. The first relates the idyllic, innocent love affair of the poet with a French girl who, under a different name, reappears in his story, "Apple Blossom in Brittany." Her age is not given; she is more than a little girl since he leads her home as his bride, but she is still very young and shy and one night her mother has to come out chiding that the grass is bright with dew. Needless to say, the lovers do not live happily ever after, since living means aging and Dowson cannot imagine age bringing anything but loss. In less than a year death separates them: "There is dew on your grave grass, Yvonne,/But your feet it shall not wet . . ." (53). Griefstricken, he mourns her in the same orchard where he has loved her; but the poem, however sad, seems to intimate that loss through death may be better than loss through growth.

The intimation becomes a direct admission in "Villanelle of Sunset," which Yeats called "perfect song," and again in "The Dead Child," where the poet stands above a grave and

cries: "Lie still and be/For evermore a child." In neither poem
does he wish to wake the child. Life would only defile what
death has somehow preserved. The two poems, in their tinkling
grace and in their theme of flowerlike children taken by death,
recall the tiny elegy of Robert Herrick, "Upon a Child That
Died": "Here she lies, a pretty bud,/Lately made of flesh
and blood. . . ."⁹ But where Herrick is content to stand at the
graveside, scattering flowers, Dowson would go a step further:
"I want to come thy way,/And share thy rest" (106). For the
Cavalier poet, in love with life and not with death, childhood
is sweet but so are the succeeding stages of human development. He mourns but he does not linger beside the grave of
youth. For Dowson childhood is the summit of life, and he
does not hesitate to follow it into the grave.

But, if death is much the most thorough solution to the
threat of age, Dowson is realist or poet enough to know that
it should not be sought too often. Yvonne and the nameless
"dead child" enjoy a profound slumber and a never-fading
childhood, but other girls must be shown as less fortunate
and as overtaken by time. Such a girl he laments in "Jadis"
("Erewhile"), a rondel, a verse form of eleven lines which
Swinburne adapted from the French rondel and which Dowson employs with apparent ease and concealed artfulness. The
insistent rhyming of "old," "enrolled," "gold," "told," and
"cold" rings in the mind like a bell remembered from Christ-
mas, and the one-word refrain, "Erewhile," tinkles like a wind
chime and fades at last into silence. The poet looks back
longingly to the time when he and his love, both children,
were enrolled in the train of Cupid. Perhaps in Italy, where
he had traveled as a boy with his parents, he had seen
Pompeian frescoes of the love god and his attendant amoretti:

> Your little hands were clasped in mine,
> Your head all ruddy and sun-gold
> Lay on my breast which was your shrine. . . .

But time intrudes, time, the merciless; and the poem ends
with the familiar burden:

> Ah, God, that sweet things should decline,
> And fires fade out which were not cold,
> Erewhile. (118)

In one poem only, "Growth," does he admit that compensation may accompany time. Having apprehensively watched his beloved grow from child to maiden, he finds to his astonishment that the "ancient good" of her childhood endures in a new disguise. She has kept, after all, her "old tenderness." But even in "Growth" childhood remains the measure of excellence, and later periods are acceptable not for their own sake but because they preserve or build upon the qualities of the child. Paralleling the theme of this poem, Dowson wrote about Adelaide to Victor Plarr: "Das Kleine [the little one] instead of changing, altering, repelling, as I feared/hoped might happen, in the nature of things, seems to grow in grace and favour daily." But he was not confident that her growth would continue for the best: "What a terrible, lamentable thing growth is! It 'makes me mad' to think that in a year or two at most the most perfect exquisite relation I ever succeeded in making must naturally end. . . ." [10]

Some critics have suspected that Dowson paid court to a child and feared her budding womanhood because he was impotent. They point to Ruskin, who was unable to consummate his marriage to Euphemia Chalmers Gray and, after their annulment, took refuge in the undemanding love of the child Rose. But Dowson was far from impotent. As we shall see, the "bought red mouth" in "Cynara" was surely not imagined. Both Pound and Yeats told the story of Dowson and Oscar Wilde visiting a brothel in France. Wilde, just out of prison, complained afterward: "The first in these ten years, and it will be the last. . . . But tell it in England, for it will entirely restore my character." Dowson had no need to restore his own reputation for manhood. It was never in doubt with those who knew him well. The truth seems to be that he felt both love and lust but drew a careful distinction between them. The first, he believed, should be altogether spiritual; thus he chose to love Adelaide, who did not arouse him physically. But though he remained faithful to her in his fashion, he satisfied his physical hungers with women of pleasure. If his separation seems rigid and unrealistic, it is nonetheless poetic. The sweet innocence of his seven child-love poems is hardly less effective than the wine-stained wickedness of "Cynara." Unlike Peter

[40]

Pan, he had to grow up, but the little world of his poems has kept his Adelaide, his Wendy, "for evermore a child."

II   *Unrequited Love*

In his poems about unrequited love, Dowson's Adelaide grows to womanhood. As a child, she was kind to him, a playmate more than a sweetheart. As a woman, she can no longer afford to be kind; she must keep him at a distance. She is not a coquette, she is never deliberately cruel, but often she ignores or rejects him and thus inflicts suffering. Aloof and self-sufficient, she walks the rarefied heights of her dream, "nor recks if she enthrall." Like the snow maiden of Hawthorne's story, she is meant to be worshiped from afar. The poems which enshrine her are constructed with the intricacy of snowflakes, as fragile and as perfect; and their central images—frost, whiteness, silver, marble—are taken from winter, its purity rather than its barrenness.

Two of them are villanelles, a difficult and decorative form which is admirably suited to the subject. In "Villanelle of His Lady's Treasures," the poet compares her voice to a silver bell and extols her "whiteness virginal." He weaves the frosty treasures of her beauty into a song with the hope that the act of singing will lessen his despair. The lady herself is unconcerned with her effect on the poet. Any salvation must be of his own making. In the similar "Villanelle of Marguerites" she walks through a meadow casting the "snowy petals" of daisies on the air. The white flower is significant; no less than the immaculate lilies of "Cynara," it symbolizes her detachment from mortal love, his love. As she scatters the petals with blithe unconcern, so she scatters his hopes. Her visions, being unworldly, are "too fair" to allow the intrusion of a worldly lover.

Other poems, not villanelles but no less graceful, present the same girl under different guises. In "Vain Resolves" he tries to forget her "passionless, pure eyes, how cold they were"; but she smiles to him out of courtesy and makes him discard his resolve. A condescending smile is the one response she is able to give. Such a smile, coming as it does from a goddess, seems to him a gift beyond measure. Had she given more than the smile—herself, perhaps—her bounty might have seemed wantonness. He prefers the condescension of a goddess to the surrender of a woman.

In "Quid Non Speremos, Amantes?" ("What Do We Not Hope For, Lovers?"), the poet has to content himself with less than a smile: with thorns. He complains that "she is cold, and vainly have we prayed," but he concludes that the thorns of love are "sweet as never roses are." He is like the self-mortifying hero of Pierre Louÿs' *The Woman and the Puppet*: the more the woman whipped and reviled him, the more the puppet loved her. The theme of the masochistic lover—first popularized by Baudelaire, Swinburne, and Sacher-Masoch—enjoyed a considerable vogue through the 1890's; but Dowson treats it with such restraint that the abnormality is not apparent.

In "Amor Umbratilis," a poem incongruously composed on the back of an unpaid bill, he concludes that self-abasement is not enough: he must altogether efface himself. He watches his beloved pass, "serene and cold," and wonders what gift to give her. He has no songs that she "should heed or know." He has cast away his flowers—his rosemary and rue—because they were "unmeet" for her. One gift alone is fitting:

> *Yea, for I cast you, sweet!*
> *This one gift, you shall take:*
> *Like ointment, on your unobservant feet,*
> *My silence, for your sake.* (48)

Though written in the early stages of his infatuation for Adelaide, "Amor Umbratilis" is the ultimate self-negation. Even his worship, he seems to say, is not worthy of her. He must therefore worship in silence. Ironically, his song of silence spoke with great eloquence to the readers of *The Century Guild Hobby Horse*, where, published in 1891, it charmed the same readers who earlier that year had sighed with "Cynara."

But Dowson is a man as well as a worshiper. While usually content to be ignored by his goddess and to keep a respectful distance, he has occasional doubts. In "Exchanges" he sighs that in return for his rhyme and roses, little enough but all he had, she did not even give him a "word compassionate." And in "A Song," he protests that he has prayed to her but still her eyes and heart remain dumb. Finally, in the grave and wistful "Terre Promise" ("Promised Land") he wonders if a touch of hand or speaking silence can win her "to droop into mine arms and understand!" No longer willing to worship her with silence, no longer satisfied with thorns or the little gift of a smile, he asks to become an equal instead of an idolater. He wishes for a woman instead of an idol. A stronger reservation, indeed a bitter one, he expresses in the six-line "Epigram." Because he has worshiped his love with single-minded devotion, the jealous gods ". . . who brook no worship save their own,/Turned my live idol marble and her heart to stone" (93). For once her coldness is repellent; her marble is not of purity but of heartlessness. "Epigram" is perhaps a warning to himself that his own worship may be turning Adelaide into stone.

At other times, instead of reproaching her for coldness, he wishes to free himself. In "Spleen" he succeeds for the space of a day and his hunger becomes oblivion, but evening restores his thralldom. In "Libera Me" ("Liberate Me"), written, surprisingly, in 1886 before he knew Adelaide, he seeks a more permanent relief. He invokes the goddess Aphrodite, and not for the gift of love:

Goddess the laughter-loving, Aphrodite befriend!
Long have I served thine altars, serve me now at the end,
Let me have peace of thee, truce of thee, golden one, send. (133)

The first line is an echo of Swinburne's "Hymn to Proserpine" ("Goddess and maiden and queen, be near me now and befriend"), and both poets have perhaps been reading Sappho, whose "Hymn to Aphrodite" enchanted the Greeks and somehow escaped the book burnings of the medieval Church to enchant the Victorians. The accents of "Libera Me" are clearly borrowed; but the speaker is Dowson, the idolater, weary of his idol and craving release.

Far more often, however, he accepts coldness as the fitting, the inevitable quality of his snow princess. "Flos Lunae" is the clearest expression of his attitude, the unequivocal admission that, in spite of momentary reservations, in spite of his occasional outcry for understanding, he would not alter her:

I would not alter thy cold eyes,
Nor trouble the calm fount of speech
With aught of passion or surprise.
The heart of thee I cannot reach:
I would not alter thy cold eyes! (57)

Yes, on the whole, his snow maiden pleases him, and he does not intend, like the children in Hawthorne's story, to take her indoors and see her melt. As Symons wrote: "In the case of Dowson and [Adelaide] . . . there was a sort of virginal devotion, as to a Madonna; and I think, had things gone happily, to a conventionally happy ending, he would have felt (dare I say?) that his ideal had been spoilt." [11]

The Adelaide of Dowson's poems is not a waitress with red hands and a crooked nose, but a girl transfigured and marbleized by art. Like a statue in the cella of a Greek temple, she is worthy of worship. But most readers will prefer the shy and modest poet who created her. They will prize the worshiped as a rare creation, cold and perfect like a Pallas by Phidias; but they will love the worshiper, and love him all the more for the human frailties which he recognized in himself and ruthlessly excluded from his marmoreal goddess.

III   Sinful Love

Dowson and "Cynara": the two have become inseparable. "The greatest poem of this time," cried Frank Harris when Dowson recited "Cynara" to him in the Cafe Royal. Its subject, like that of the poems just treated, is unrequited love; Cynara's rejection of the poet, apparently, has driven him to his wine and harlots. But as Dowson's most famous poem, it demands to be quoted in full and treated in separate eminence:

Last night, ah, yesternight, betwixt her lips and mine
There fell thy shadow, Cynara! thy breath was shed
Upon my soul between the kisses and the wine;
And I was desolate and sick of an old passion,
    Yea, I was desolate and bowed my head:
I have been faithful to thee, Cynara! in my fashion.

All night upon mine heart I felt her warm heart beat,
Night-long within mine arms in love and sleep she lay;

> Surely the kisses of her bought red mouth were sweet;
> But I was desolate and sick of an old passion,
>   When I awoke and found the dawn was gray:
> I have been faithful to thee, Cynara! in my fashion.
>
> I have forgot much, Cynara! gone with the wind,
> Flung roses, roses riotously with the throng,
> Dancing, to put thy pale, lost lilies out of mind;
> But I was desolate and sick of an old passion,
>   Yea, all the time, because the dance was long:
> I have been faithful to thee, Cynara! in my fashion.
>
> I cried for madder music and for stronger wine,
> But when the feast is finished and the lamps expire,
> Then falls thy shadow, Cynara! the night is thine;
> And I am desolate and sick of an old passion,
>   Yea, hungry for the lips of my desire:
> I have been faithful to thee, Cynara! in my fashion. (58)

Dowson himself thought "Cynara" the best of his poems. If friends could persuade him to overcome his shyness, he liked to recite it, as he did to Harris, in a low, musical monotone. First published in *The Century Guild Hobby Horse* (1891), a magazine which served as a link between the Pre-Raphaelites and the 1890's, "Cynara" drew immediate praise. Symons wrote nine years later, after Dowson's death: "In the lyric in which he has epitomized himself and his whole life, a lyric which is certainly one of the greatest lyrical poems of our time . . . he has for once said everything, and he has said it to an intoxicating and perhaps immortal music." A kind of heartcry of Decadence, the poem was memorized, quoted, and anthologized until the refrain "faithful in my fashion" became a popular phrase and Cynara (her name mispronounced with emphasis on the second instead of the first syllable) a familiar heroine of literature. A phrase from the third stanza, "gone with the wind," reappeared in 1939 as the title of a famous book.

What was the inspiration for the poem? Dowson's original title read "Non Sum Qualis Eram Bonae Sub Regno Cynarae," a line from the First Ode of the Fourth Book of Horace which may be translated, "I am not what once I was in kind Cynara's day." Latin poetry often gave Dowson subjects, but he freely adapted them to express his own experience. As Symons wrote, "He used the commonplaces of poetry frankly, making them his own by his belief in them: the Horatian Cynara or Neobule was still the natural symbol for him when he wished to be most personal." [12]

It is easy to find parallels between "Cynara" and Dowson's life. He wrote the poem in a London ale house called the "Cock," on scraps of paper and table tops; probably he had drunk the "stronger wine" and cried for the "madder music" in that very bar. As for the "bought red mouth," his affairs with harlots are well authenticated. In London he consorted with a woman named Dulcie, who was not above stripping off her clothes to attract attention, and a slightly more decorous Essie, who had come to town from the provinces. According to Yeats, Dowson was seen in France with an even more common harlot. Half drunk at the time, he protested in her defense: "She writes poetry—it is like Browning and Mrs. Browning." [13] While he had not yet met these particular women when he wrote "Cynara," he doubtless knew others like them. Finally and most important, who was the lady of the title? Some critics identify her with Adelaide. Others reply that Adelaide was only twelve years old at the time and that Dowson had not known her long enough to develop an "old passion." But, if not Adelaide herself, his inspiration was probably an ideal of innocence which he soon came to identify with her.

Regardless of the model for Cynara, the poem is important as the heartcry of Decadence. The mood of despair, epitomized in the line "When I awoke and found the dawn was gray," is characteristic of the period. The past, once bright, is irretrievable, the poet seems to say. The present is barren and hopeless. What is life but memories and drugged forgetfulness, bought love, and ever stronger wine? Decadent too are the richly symbolic flowers, the rose as an emblem of vice, the lily as an emblem of virtue. In Dowson's poem roses are flung by the throng to deck the path of sin, while pale, lost lilies symbolize the innocence of Cynara. Finally, the Decadents liked to proclaim their love—or lust—for harlots. It was a way of attacking the Victorian prudery which they despised, the maidenliness of poets like Tennyson, and the stuffiness of critics and editors. Wilde wrote a poem about a harlot's house; Symons paid affectionate tribute to Emmy, who told "tale after shameless tale"; and Dowson intimates a night in the arms of a woman he has bought to help him forget his Cynara.

The poem also illustrates the painstaking craftsmanship of the Decadent era. Dowson chose for his meter the difficult Alexandrine, a line of six iambic feet, often found in the French romances of the twelfth and thirteenth centuries and also in Baudelaire, Rimbaud, and Verlaine; but a meter which was rare and usually unsuccessful in English. In the hands of most English poets, hexameters either break in half or look like overblown pentameters. Dowson avoided both weaknesses. His lines exist as perfect units in themselves and yet they flow into the larger units of the four stanzas. Each stanza contains six lines, the fifth line a pentameter for the sake of variety, the fourth and sixth lines identical or almost identical with corresponding lines in the other stanzas. The rhyme words of the two repeated lines, "passion" and "fashion," help with their slight inexactness to vary the exactness of the other rhymes and, like the occasional pentameters, to avoid the monotony of excessive smoothness.

Some critics, it must be admitted, cannot read "Cynara" without wincing. They shudder at the archaisms, "betwixt" and "yesternight," and insist that the entire poem is theatrical rather than convincing, a calculated gesture rather than a sincere heartcry. Passion should be intimated, not shouted, they insist, intellectualized, not emotionalized. They prefer the bud to the full-blown rose. Unquestionably "Cynara" is old-fashioned. But it is wrong to call a poem faded when it is merely out of critical fashion. "Cynara" remains a passionate poem about real passion. The archaic words are appropriate because the poet loves with the weight of centuries upon him. He is Horace as well as Dowson; his love is also the Roman Cynara. Yesternight is last night and was also last night two thousand years ago. As Victor Plarr has written, with an eye to Propertius instead of Horace: "There is a singular, a poignant parellelism between the great and prolonged *cri du coeur* of the old Roman and the modern's sorrowful lament, as expressed, for instance in [Dowson's] Cynara poem, the bold-

ness of which is august with the spirit of antiquity, as though
the pagan had passed into and inspired the unhappy lad of
the day before yesterday." [14]

To appreciate the authentic passion of "Cynara," it is interesting to read for contrast a poem about synthetic passion,
Symons' "Hallucinations":

> One petal of a blood-red tulip pressed
> Between the pages of a Baudelaire:
> No more; and I was suddenly aware
> Of the white fragrant apple of a breast
> On which my lips were pastured. . . .[15]

The details are shrewdly chosen, too shrewdly: the tulip, red
like passion; a book by the amorous author of *The Flowers of
Evil*; and the extravagant image of lips pasturing on the "fra-
grant apple of a breast." Such calculated eroticism, frequent
in Symons and Swinburne, is absent from "Cynara," in which
even the "bought red mouth" is appropriate under the circumstances. Dowson does not falsify in order to achieve a theatrical
effect, erotic or otherwise. That he sought such effect is denied
by his remark, after seeing the poem in proof: "It looks less
indecent in print, but I am still nervous!" [16]

Whether Cynara herself was Adelaide or an ideal, Dowson
has made her real, not in the sense that we can picture her
walking in Piccadilly or Times Square; but, like the Laura
of Petrarch and the Cynthia of Propertius, she is larger than
life and therefore timeless. His poem sighs and then it sings
with a mournful and indeed immortal music. The pale lost lilies
and the scattered roses have not begun to wilt.

IV   Threatened Love

The grass grows to be cut by the scythe; the rosebud swells
to the flower and drops its petals: and man, wherever he looks,
must read presentiments of his own doom. But proud in spite
of his transience, he can fling a protest in the teeth of time.
One such protest is the *carpe diem* song, a kind of lyric, part
of a long tradition, in which the poet says to his sweetheart:
love me because today is good and tomorrow we die. The song
is at least as old as Horace, who originated the phrase "*carpe
diem*" or "seize the day" in his ode to Leuconoë: "So seize the

day, or ever it be past/And let the morrow come for what it will." [17] In the seventeenth century the Cavalier poets of England—Herrick, Waller, Carew, Lovelace, and Suckling—repeated and enlivened the pleas of Horace, and Andrew Marvell sang to his coy mistress: "The grave's a fine and private place,/But none I think do there embrace." [18]

To the same tradition, surprisingly, belong six poems by Dowson, who borrows the name Lalage from Horace, mourns with Herrick the loss of roses, and echoes Marvell in dreading the passionless grave. But Dowson sang *carpe diem* with a difference. He disliked life even while he lamented its passing. Horace, the Cavalier poets, and Marvell could fret and groan and complain of love's alarms, but they valued life in spite of its liabilities. They believed in the preciousness of the moment, and their poems show immense vitality. Who can doubt that, when Herrick bids the virgins to gather rosebuds, he thinks those buds worth gathering? Who can miss Marvell's joy in the lines:

> Let us roll all our Strength and all
> Our sweetness up into one Ball,
> And tear our Pleasures with rough strife
> Through the iron gates of Life. . . .[19]

Marvell and Herrick may prove inconstant lovers, but the day itself, in its flowers and sun and softness, they prize with all their hearts. To Dowson, however, the day is not sweet for its own sake, which seems negligible, but because the winter which follows is worse. In other words, youth, beauty, and spring are desirable only because they are better than age, ugliness, and winter. Reflecting this view of life, darkness and languor dominate his *carpe diem* poems.

One of his poems, it is true, seems almost Cavalier. In "Amantium Irae" ("The Angers of the Loving"), whose title he took from Terence, *Andria*, Act III, Scene 2, he cries to his prideful sweetheart:

> While roses deck the garden,
> While yet the sun is high,
> Doff sorry pride for pardon,
> Or ever love go by. (85)

"Gather ye rose-buds while ye may," sang Herrick in a similar poem, "To the Virgins, to Make Much of Time," because the "glorious lamp of heaven," the sun, "will soon have run its race." Both poems have an effortless falling into place of the perfect rhyme word; a lilting rhythm which helps to keep the theme of transience from becoming lugubrious; and, above all, a view of the world as a place of sunlight and roses. But "Amantium Irae" is not characteristic of Dowson's *carpe diem* songs. Decidedly atypical, it suggests that even a sorrowful poet may remember how to smile. When Adelaide was kind to Dowson, he rejoiced for hours, if not days. Then his sun was high and roses, instead of being trampled like those in "Cynara," decked his garden.

At first glance "Wisdom" seems also Cavalier. The springtime of life is good, the poet implies:

> *Love wine and beauty and the spring*
> *While wine is red and spring is here*
> *And through the almond blossoms ring*
> *The dove-like voices of thy dear.* (136)

But the second stanza rejects the implication: far from good, spring is a hypocrite who masks her treachery in a smile. Embrace her only because her deceit is hidden and therefore tolerable; only because for the moment she is the best of life's bad choices. When she goes, do not lament her.

In "Amor Profanus" he makes no attempt to conceal or withhold his pessimism. The first three stanzas, in fact, describe the grave as a "world forgotten of the sun," lightless and without birds. Like Eliot's Hollow Men, his lovers stammer in vain and cannot communicate with each other. Though the last stanza alludes to "pretty, fleeting flowers," to a "little path of light," and to a mistress with "beauty rose and white," the closing lines revert to gloom:

> *For all too soon we twain shall tread*
> *The bitter pastures of the dead:*
> *Estranged, sad spectres of the night.* (50)

Clearly the poet does not so much love life as he fears death. To win his beloved's acceptance, he threatens her with future pain more than he cajoles her with promises of present bliss.

"Cease Smiling, Dear, a Little While Be Sad" is also a gloomy poem, in spite of the epigraph from Propertius, Book II, xv, 23, "While the fates allow us, let us feast our eyes with love." Not only does gloom darken the future, but the poet does his best to inflict it on the present. Though he calls youth "divine," he speaks of young love's sorrows, not its joys. In the very garden of love he tells his sweetheart to cease smiling, and he wishes to reap death from her lips in a kiss. He is like a gardener who plants weeds along with his roses so that he will not have too much beauty to lose when frost arrives. As Housman wrote in "Terence, This Is Stupid Stuff," one way to prepare for big sorrows is to immunize oneself with little sorrows even if it means deliberately cultivating them.

"Villanelle of the Poet's Road" is written in the same mood. Posing as a wise, experienced cynic, he advises young men to gather "wine and woman and song" while they may, but cautions them that in spite of these allurements life is tediously long. This somber villanelle, together with the poet's other uses of old French verse forms, led Katherine Bregy to write: "Not one of his contemporaries (not even the delectable Austin Dobson!) knew better how to use the airy and archaic beauty of these delicate verse forms. But where Dobson has used them for blithness, the younger, sadder Dowson made them serve a haunting and persistent melancholy." [20] Here is no Dobson remembering a fan that belonged to Madame Pompadour or celebrating Rose, the queen of coquettes, but a disillusioned lover who adds, after recommending the three time-tested pleasures of the poet: "Yet is day overlong."

All in all, Dowson's *carpe diem* songs make a poor case for seizing the day. The day he offers is not in itself a blessing but the lesser of two evils; at best it is better than death. He dared not argue too winningly because, had his love accepted his invitation, he could not have continued to respect her. As we have seen, he contrived one reason after another why his goddess, his Adelaide, should not submit to him, since submission entailed an abdication of divinity, a yielding to an errant mortal. If Dowson and Herrick had wooed the same mistress, there would be little doubt of her choice.

In other poems, in other contexts, Dowson treats pessimism

with supreme effectiveness. "Cynara" triumphs in its lordly anguish. But his *carpe diem* songs, except for "Amantium Irae," make the mistake of casting twilight across midmorning, of darkening a tradition which, ever since Horace, has been characterized by wit, liveliness, and life. As Miss Bregy remarked of the villanelle, these poems of Dowson possess a haunting music which never falters; if they sometimes wail, at least they never screech. But as long as the robins and rosebuds of Herrick twinkle in the sunlight, it is hard to be satisfied with nightjars.

V *Lost Love*

In the poems about unrequited love, the snow maiden kept to her mountain, and the *carpe diem* songs were hardly persuasive enough to lure her down the slopes. In a few poems, however, she tires of the frost and risks the fires of human commerce. But Dowson is vigilant. When he tolerates her descent, he does not allow her time enough in which to melt. He hurries to separate her from his own contamination. In "Exceeding Sorrow," originally titled "O Mors! Quam Amara Est Memoria Tua Homini Pacem Habenti In Substantiis Suis," they are sharing a day of love; she plays a viol for his pleasure. Then the day is threatened. The original title, taken from the Vulgate, Ecclesiasticus 41:1, may be translated, "Oh Death, How Bitter Is Your Memory to a Man Holding Peace in His Possession," but in the poem death is anticipated instead of remembered: the death of separation. Cease playing, he tells her, and "lay thine head my way" because tomorrow "we must depart." Again in "A Valediction," whose theme is that of Donne in "A Valediction Forbidding Mourning," but whose manner is more direct, he says to his love:

> *If we must part,*
> *Then let it be like this;*
> *Not heart on heart,*
> *Nor with the useless anguish of a kiss;*
> *But touch mine hand and say:*
> "Until tomorrow or some other day,
> If we must part." (88)

Both poems are written with bare simplicity and almost without images. They do not glitter with colors or ring with sounds. They do not intoxicate the senses with wine and roses like "Cynara" or lull them with shadows and incense like "Benedictio Domini." But human beings, in the stress of feeling, may speak a language whose strong, straightforward verbs and unadorned adjectives rise to eloquence. It is such a language which Dowson has caught in these poems. In spite of their passion, however, in spite of their protestations, they suggest a truth about the poet: that he secretly welcomes parting to restore the inviolateness of his heroine. When the day's kisses end in a clasp of hands, his maiden can return to the frost. She has strayed from her mountaintop but the poet himself will help her to return.

Three of Dowson's poems begin not before but after the separation of the lovers. "Impenitentia Ultima," "Seraphita," and "Exile" portray the poet as long divided from his love; years perhaps have passed since their last meeting; miles and unnamed obstacles keep them from meeting now. In the first he prays to God that before he dies he may enjoy the "little grace of an hour" reunited with his sweetheart. (Of this poem, Frank Harris remarked: "the hands are the hands of Dowson but the voice is the voice of Swinburne.")[21] In the second he asks even less. For an unstated reason he cannot hope to see her face to face again (it is possible that she is dead, since he speaks of the "serenity of thine abiding-place"). But he begs her image to come before him in his final "great despair." In the third he asks for nothing. Without hope and without protest, he yields himself to the "sad waters of separation." [22]

Three additional poems speak not of lovers separated but of love which has died. Dowson has found in these poems a surer means to restore and preserve his heroine's purity, since miles can be crossed but a dead love is hard to revive. In "The Garden of Shadow" the perfect flowers have not yet felt the death of spring, but love has grown blind, ". . . with no more count of hours,/ Nor part in seed-time nor in harvesting" (79). In "To a Lost Love," whose title states its subject, he confesses, "I knew the end before the end was nigh." Again in the rondel "Beyond," which he wrote to an unidentifiable woman named Hélène,[23] he sighs:

> *Love's aftermath! I think the time is now*
> *That we must gather in, alone, apart*
> *The saddest crop of all the crops that grow,*
> *Love's aftermath.* (99)

Lovers though parted may reunite. Love though dead may be resurrected. But a sure way to preserve the inviolateness of a heroine is to kill her. She can stray from a mountaintop but not from the grave. In "Vanitas" she has gone to "oblivious lands" whose cypress is sweeter than the laurels of the living. The poet grieves for her and imagines a future meeting across the "weary river." All the same, he does not regret her death. "Beyond the reach of hands," his hands, she is also beyond the reach of contaminating love. In the similar but stronger "You Would Have Understood Me, Had You Waited," he takes his epigraph from Verlaine's "Reversibility": "Ah, in these sad sojourns/The Nevers are the Always." Pride and impatience have kept him from his love. Now she is dead:

> *I would not waken you: nay! this is fitter;*
> *Death and the darkness give you unto me;*
> *Here we who loved so, were so cold and bitter,*
> *Hardly can disagree.* (66)

After "Cynara" and "Vita Summa Brevis . . . ," "You Would Have Understood Me" is probably his most popular and most often anthologized poem. Mark Longaker has predicted that "time and sea-change" will only add to its beauty. It is Dowson at his best. His favorite flower, the rose, enwreathes the grave of the heroine; his favorite themes, love and death, intermingle and fuse to the mournful enrichment of both, the second preserving the first. If his maiden seems a little quarrelsome and less than her usual perfection, she gains a humanity she enjoys in no other poem. The verse form is simple and appropriate: seven quatrains of iambic pentameter alternating, in every fourth line, with iambic trimeter. A more elaborate form—for example, the villanelle—would have seemed at variance with the quietly grieving lover and the simple finalities of the grave. As in some of the poems about children, death and the darkness give her unto him.

[54]

For Love of Adelaide

Readers have protested the severity of Dowson's ideal in "You Would Have Understood Me" and other poems, and complained that his lovers seem separated less by fate than the inclination of the poet. But the poet's dogged insistence on rejection and separation, on forebodings and farewells, however unsatisfying to the romanticist, is a part of his individuality, his difference from other poets. He has fashioned a goddess, aloof and virginal; and he will not see her profaned by himself or other men. She may sometimes chill, but she meets a lasting need in human nature. We live in a workaday world of change and imperfection. To escape at times, to seek unchanging perfection, is not a weakness but a necessity, and Dowson has given us a place in which to look. He found a girl, average if not inferior, and raised her into a goddess. A poet as well as a dreamer, he gave her the sanctuary of his poems; and, like William Morris, he opened the ivory gate for others to follow him.

CHAPTER 3

The Hollow Land

L IKE MOST lyric poets, Dowson found material in whatever
moved his heart; and love, though his most important, was
not his only subject. Nature, death, religion, and a loosely
defined subject which can best be termed escape also inspired
him, and he treated them with skill in a variety of forms and
unified them with a single mood of despair. His predominant
landscape, described or implied, abhorred or frantically fled,
is one we have met in some of his love poems, a hollow land
of birdless deserts and cities which are ruled by ghosts; the
land which Christina Rossetti had visited in "The Prince's
Progress" and Browning in "Childe Roland to the Dark Tower
Came," and which Eliot was later to visit in "The Hollow
Men" and *The Waste Land*. Without the sustaining faith
of Browning and Miss Rossetti, without the faint hope, even,
of the disillusioned young Eliot, Dowson can only sigh—and
dream.

Though love is no longer preeminent, Adelaide remains—in-
visible at times but potent. Nature reflects the poet's melancholy, which grows, as often as not, from his unrequited love.
Ecstatic because of love, he fears to die; anguished, he wishes
to die. Religion helps to solace his broken heart, and escape
offers an alternative to loving an image of snow. In the hollow
land, it may be love which casts the longest shadow; and, when
he escapes to the land where he is not, it may be love which
drives him to flight.

I *Nature*

"Of modern science," wrote Victor Plarr, with particular
reference, no doubt, to biology, Dowson "knew nothing at

all," [1] and he adds in a later passage: "Ernest Dowson in the country was a delight. Seeing an innocent newt walking out slowly on the sandy road . . . he announced with horror that the newt was a serpent, and arming himself with a large stake . . . he proceeded to belabour the little creature, which ended by being banged down, quite unscathed, in the deep sand. He made me get another stick in case we met more dangerous reptiles." [2] After a second visit into the wilds, this time with his friend Conal O'Riordan in France, Dowson retreated to Paris because "the country quiet was too much for him. He said he was afraid he might marry a dairymaid." [3] He was not at ease out-of-doors. He did not, like the Impressionist painters, sit in a forest and study the play of light on leaves or, like the Georgian poets, detail the countryside with loving accuracy. He more or less agreed with Huysmans' hero, Des Esseintes:

> As he used to say, Nature has had her day; she has definitely and finally tired out by the sickening monotony of her landscapes and skyscapes the patience of refined temperaments. When all is said and done, what a narrow, vulgar affair it all is, like a petty shopkeeper selling one article of goods to the exclusion of all others; what a tiresome store of green fields and leafy trees, what a wearisome commonplace collection of mountains and seas!
>
> .   .   .   .   .
>
> Yes, there is no denying it, she is in her dotage and has long ago exhausted the simple-minded admiration of the true artist; the time is undoubtedly come when her productions must be superseded by art. [4]

Yet much of Dowson's imagery is drawn from nature. Birds trill in his poems, boughs twine, roses and lilies flourish or fade. Where did he get them? Like most of the Decadents, Wilde in particular, he got them from books. His favorite line of poetry was one by Poe, "the viol, the violet, and the vine," and he scattered both violets and vines through "A Coronal" (which he wrote in less than an hour):

> *Violets and leaves of vine*
> *For Love that lives a day,*
> *We gather and entwine.* [5]

Roses from the odes of Horace pleased him more than those which might have grown in his garden—had he kept a garden—and he flung them riotously through "Cynara." When he writes of the ocean in "Sea-Change," it is not with the firsthand knowledge of a sailor or even of an observant passenger, but with unmistakable echoes of Swinburne's "Triumph of Time."

It does not follow, however, that because he borrowed from books he wrote about nature badly. Whether he planted violets in his garden and observed their color and configuration is less important than the use he made of them in his poems. One use is purely decorative. He liked some words for their sound. "V" was his favorite letter, and when "violet" and "vine" appear in the same line, the effect is sweetly alliterative. More important, nature becomes a mirror for his melancholy. "Sea-Change," for example, though it echoes Swinburne, speaks for Dowson at the same time: he hopes to merge with the salt embrace of the ocean until "the weary ways of men and one woman I shall forget." The woman is Adelaide.

Much of his most frequent nature imagery is drawn from the seasons. Often he names a month or a season either in his title ("Autumnal") or in the poem itself ("The air is soft with the sweet May showers"), and then he develops his images accordingly: "young, green grass" for spring; "gold and green" for summer; "pale amber sunlight" for autumn; "frozen hills" for winter. Almost always his use of seasons is symbolic: his poems symbolize the seasons in each man's life and heart, and they seem to say that youth and love, like spring, are brief and irrecoverable.

He wrote one or more poems for each season. Of his three poems about spring, "April Love," "In Spring," and "My Lady April," the third is much the best and also the best example of his symbolism. First published in *Temple Bar* (1889), the magazine which the previous year had printed "Souvenirs of an Egotist," his first short story, "My Lady April" personifies the month as a lady "full of all feathered sweetness," who passes with dainty step, singing. But "traces of tears her languid lashes wear." Does she weep, he asks, because she foresees "Autumn and withered leaves and vanity,/And winter bringing end in barrenness" (45)? Here is the insistent theme of his poems about the seasons: as spring foresees winter, so youth foresees old age. The form of the poem is an old and, by Dowson's time, almost faded one: the Italian or Petrarchan sonnet. And, at first glance, his personification of April as a young woman seems no more resourceful than the form. April's fresh green leaflets, pink buds, and melodious birds obviously suggest a singing maiden, just as frost and snow suggest a grizzled old man. But Dowson's April, in spite of her song, is not the lady of other poets. Her difference is her sadness. He has darkened her with his own melancholy, his own refusal to enjoy the present because he divines the future. Mingling lightness and sorrow, she is a kind of seasonal *Dame aux Camellias* who laughs gaily in company but when no one is watching dabs at her cheek with a handkerchief. If she is not the joyous singer of earlier poets, neither is she the idiot April of Edna St. Vincent Millay, "babbling and strewing flowers." Dowson's despair is rarely tinged with the cynicism and irony of twentieth-century poets. He sighs but he does not rage or censure. His poem lacks the scorching power of Miss Millay's "Spring" (and also of Eliot's famous passage in *The Waste Land* beginning, "April is the cruellest month. . . ."), but more than compensates in wistful delicacy. We can share his lady's tears because they are troubling presentiments of our own transcience.

In "Saint Germain-en-Laye," which takes its title from a heavily forested commune just north of Paris, summer is also personified. We are not told the sex, but the phrase "the glory of thine head" implies a girl or a woman (or possibly a long-haired youth in the style of Botticelli). As the poet speaks, he confronts the "white, gaunt" ghost of summer and grieves that summer herself has long since fled to some "far night," along with his own youth and dreams. Though published in the prestigious *Savoy*, "Saint Germain-en-Laye" pales beside "My Lady April" because the personification of summer is less exact, less touchingly human than that of spring. We miss the pathos of the lady with tears. Furthermore, a single sentence is allowed to run through eight lines, with confusing punctuation and syntax, and the poem ends with the poet-worn phrase, "golden dreams." Still, the theme is typical of Dowson. He is so conscious of summer's quick departure that he imagines her as already departed and admits that, even while she was here, "through the green boughs I hardly saw thy face. . . ."

In his poem about the fall, "Autumnal," he seems at first to enjoy a season without dreading the future. Enfolded by autumn, he rejoices that ". . . summer's loss/Seems little, dear! on days like these!" But the threat of winter is soon intimated: "Our love, a twilight of the heart/Eludes a little time's deceit" (74). And the last stanza discloses autumn in all her brief fragility as a "poor hour of ease," with winter, hushed but unhidden, threatening the ultimate frost. Yes, autumn must die, together with autumnal love; and the poet mourns even while he loves. The first stanza suffers from the hackneyed rhyming of "trees" and "breeze," but succeeding stanzas build to a gently insistent dirge whose phrases, like falling leaves, drift in the mind and settle at last into silence.

The winter poem, "Moritura," was published in March, 1887, during his first year at Oxford. His second published poem, it represents—in the words of Longaker—"one of his earliest attempts to make articulate a sentiment to which he remained faithful to the end," [6] a recurrent pessimism. The "old, old man" who "stands and mumbles" is Dowson himself as he fears to become in the future. Technically the poem is poor. The very young poet has not yet learned to match his rhythm to his subject: the jingling lines and the many exclamation points noisily seem to deny the title, which means "dying," and the stated theme of loss and decay. But the theme is nonetheless plain: all things end in winter.

Dowson and the other Decadents, coming as they did in a highly civilized and increasingly mechanized era, were in no sense lovers of nature. They were dreamers, not doers; readers and talkers, not walkers; they mused, meditated, and brooded; they would rather meet in a pub than cultivate roses or ramble through blackberry thickets. Brandy and absinthe scented the air they breathed, not dogwood. Still, they were poets, and poets need symbols to show their moods and conditions: symbols more varied and permanent than those of the city and the tavern. As Dowson recognized, cities change and the poetry which reflects them dates; but roses and lilies are older than civilization and probably more enduring. Wishing his poems to endure beyond the limits of his own life, he resorted to a nature which he found in books and he borrowed her images to mirror his melancholy. His frequent success is the triumph of first-rate art over secondhand knowledge.

II *Death*

No other English poets have been so preoccupied with death as the Decadents of the 1890's, and no Decadent wrote about death so often as Ernest Dowson. We have seen the shadow of death in some of his love poems to Adelaide, and again in the nature poems where it waits at the end of autumn. But in ten of his poems, the shadow becomes a presence. In four, the presence is evil or at least unwanted. In six, it is strangely welcome, a last assuagement to the fever of living and almost, at times, a lover to be wooed, like the "white death" of Swinburne's "Rondel," for the sweetness of his final kiss.

When death is evil, the poet resists him through love. In "Sapientia Lunae" the wisdom of the world says, "Go forth and run, the race is to the brave," but the wisdom of the moon warns him that he shall become the "worms' sweet food." Accepting the moon's word rather than the world's, he consoles himself with the "golden face" of his beloved. But love is not always so dependable. In "Gray Nights," which he wrote "after consuming many whiskeys" (220), he enters the country of death wth his beloved and watches the light of affection fade from her eyes. He flings his memories after the ghost of love. Again in "Dregs," a brief requiem perhaps inspired by a line from Swinburne, "This is the end of every man's desire," love has companioned him for part of his journey, and the ghost of love a little longer; but then comes the "dropt curtain and the closing gate," when even ghosts are forgotten.

Love at best, the poet seems to say, is a doubtful refuge; death must prevail against all resistance. Perhaps the most sensible course, then, is resignation. Dowson resigns himself in his second most familiar poem, "Vitae Summa Brevis Spem Nos Vetat Incohare Longam," whose title he found in the Fourth Ode of Book One of Horace: "The sum total of life, brief as it is, forbids us to begin the long hope." Dowson's poem in turn supplied the title for a famous television play, afterward a book and a movie, *The Days of Wine and Roses*:

They are not long, the weeping and the laughter,
 Love and desire and hate:
I think they have no portion in us after
 We pass the gate.

They are not long, the days of wine and roses:
 Out of a misty dream
Our path emerges for a while, then closes
 Within a dream. (38)

The plainest words and rhymes; a single adjective, "misty," and
a list of familiar nouns; a straightforward statement that the
days of wine and roses, into which we emerge from a dream,
close in a dream—of such simplicity Dowson has woven a
classic. He does not strive after bold or novel expression. He
avoids the high-flown phrases of "Cynara," which, supremely
effective in that very different poem, would here have proved
disastrous, a fustian attempt to disguise an old and familiar
subject. But simplicity can become banality. How does he
avoid the banal? We have often been told, by Longfellow
and others, that life is real and men should recognize its
meaning and its dignity; we have also been told that life is
an empty vessel and men should be sad or resentful. Dowson,
on the other hand, states without exhorting, without preaching.
He leaves us to draw our own conclusion, and his poem succeeds through its self-effacing modesty.

In "Sapientia Lunae," "Gray Nights," and "Dregs," the poet
resists death; in "Vitae Summa Brevis . . ." he resigns himself;
but more of his poems treat death as a state like Nirvana,
that is consciously to be welcomed. In "Vesperal," professing
to speak for other men as well as himself, he says that life is
"labour and longing and despair" and at the end we "are not
loth" to receive the poppies of death. In "Villanelle of
Acheron," which takes its title from the river in Hades, he
hails the goddess of Swinburne, the dark Proserpine whose
gift is immortal sleep. In "A Breton Cemetery" he envies the
fisherfolk who have escaped into the grave from "fierce Atlantic ways." Like them, he is tempest-tossed, and they beckon
him to their lands of peace. A fourth poem, "A Requiem,"
expresses the same theme and also illustrates his method of

altering Classical materials to his own purpose. He addresses Neobule, a girl unhappy in life and blessed by death:

> *Neobule, being tired,*
> *Far too tired to laugh or weep,*
> *From the hours, rosy and gray,*
> *Hid her golden face away.*
> *Neobule, fain of sleep,*
> *Slept at last as she desired!* (70)

The name of the girl is Roman; he found her in the Twelfth Ode, Book Three, of Horace. But Horace's Neobule was very different. She was, it is true, unhappy; she had fallen in love with Hebrus, the "bright Liparaean"; but she did not die nor wish to die. Her wretchedness seems to have been the passing kind endured and half enjoyed by most young girls. Dowson has adapted a Horatian heroine to accommodate his own death wish; burdened her with his own weariness. As he mourns at Neobule's grave, it is clear that he wishes to join her.

In "A Requiem" he envies a dead maiden, but in "Venite Descendamus" ("Come, Let Us Descend") the maiden is not only very much alive but also the reason he wishes to die. She has scorned him, his lute, and his songs. Like Thomas Wyatt crying, "My lute, be still, for I have done," he cries to himself and his music:

> *Let be at last; give over words and sighing,*
> *Vainly were all things said:*
> *Better at last to find a place for lying,*
> *Only dead.* (127)

In 1893, the year before she died, Christina Rossetti wrote:

> *Sleeping at last, the trouble and tumult over,*
> *Sleeping at last, the struggle and horror past,*
> *Cold and white, out of sight of friend and of lover,*
> *Sleeping at last.*[7]

Dowson, who liked Miss Rossetti's work and who might have read her poem when it appeared in *New Poems* the same year

(1896) he published "Venite Descendamus" in *The Savoy,* resembles her in his death wish. While still a girl she had written a curiously happy song about death, "When I Am Dead, My Dearest." But Miss Rossetti was not a Decadent poet. Beyond decay, she believed, the body was resurrected in heaven. While "Sleeping At Last" and the early song do not look further than the grave, numerous other poems, among them the sonnet "Rest," affirm her belief that "when she wakes she will not think it long." To Miss Rossetti death seemed a positive good, a restful night which ended in morning; to Dowson, a negative good, a night with no awakening. His despair, more profound than hers and without the hope of resurrection, allowed him no *Sing-Songs* or "Goblin Markets."

"A Last Word," written perhaps in 1886 but printed as the last poem in his final volume of verse, epitomizes his death wish. The "perverse and aimless band" anticipate Eliot's more famous Hollow Men. Like Eliot's scarecrows, they endure the living death which is life and covet the real death of the grave. Their last words are: ". . . O pray the earth enfold/Our life-sick hearts and turn them into dust." Where Eliot fragments his verse to suggest the fragmentation of modern man, where he mingles snatches of prayer with distortions of an old nursery rhyme and jolts the reader from line to line and stanza to stanza without transitions, Dowson works instead within the tight containment of a Petrarchan sonnet; his words are measured, his thought unbroken. And yet he achieves the same funereal effect. His lines glide like the barge of Charon with its freight of corpses. His very smoothness, far from denying the nature of his subject, seems to say: the forms which enclose chaos need not be chaotic.

Taken together, Dowson's poems about death resemble a necropolis "forgotten of the sun." Darkness broods above them "like an owl" until the reader may wish for a meadowlark or, if there must be night birds, a nightingale. Death ends everything, the poet says, and what is life but a waiting to die? He was biased, of course, by his own personal tragedies, ill health, the death of his parents, and Adelaide's marriage to a rival. But his poems, however biased, sincerely reflect his beliefs. Optimism seemed dishonest to him. How then could he write optimistic poems? He might have sung "God's in his heaven" with Browning's Pippa. He might have written poems which confessed his despair but in which he hoped, with Tennyson, to see his maker face to face or cried with Richard LeGallienne, "Yet Christ is with me all the day." Had he followed either course he would doubtless have found a more immediate market and audience, and toward the end of his life he desperately needed to supplement his small income. Instead, he chose to become the most heavyhearted poet of his decade. His city, like that of James Thomson, belongs to dreadful night. But he raised her spires with the highest resources of his art, with the desperation and yet the painstaking precision of a man who wished them to outlive their builder. He built with black marble. His best poems about death—"Vitae Summa Brevis . . ." and "The Last Word" at the very least—are faultless of their kind. It is not necessary to agree with their theme in order to admire their honesty and their surpassing artistry.

III *Religion*

"My childhood was pagan," wrote Ernest Dowson, and natural religion was a "phase, which at no time of my life have I ever undergone or understood." [8] Though his parents were nominal Anglicans, he was never indoctrinated with a Christian code of ethics or instilled with a belief in heaven. If he feared no future punishment for his sins, he expected no future reward for his virtues. In *The Greek Anthology* the poet Kallimachos addresses a dead man: "Oh Charidas, what of the world below?" And Charidas answers: "A great dark." [9] Kallimachos' dialogue also speaks for Dowson, whose reading of Horace, Propertius, and Catullus could only confirm his early inclination. If William Morris was a dreamer of dreams born out of his due time, Dowson was a pagan in the same predicament: a Greek or a Roman misplaced in a Christian world. And yet he sometimes wrote about the Catholic Church. In his story "The Diary of a Successful Man" he describes the interior of the Church of the Dames Rouges in Bruges, and he quotes from the Latin service. In another story, "Apple Blossom in Brittany," he calls the convent a "gracious choice, a generous effort after perfection." In his poem "Vesperal" the Angelus consoles him for the "day's evil things," and "Breton Afternoon" closes with a prayer to Mary: "Mother of God, O Misericord, look down in pity on us . . ." (126). Four of his poems, in addition, are wholly concerned with the Church: "Nuns of the Perpetual Adoration," "Benedictio Domini," "Carthusians," and "Extreme Unction."

The four poems have sometimes been taken, together with the poet's official conversion to Catholicism in 1891, to indicate a renunciation of his paganism. But the pessimism and nihilism of his other and nonreligious poems, with their references to the cold finality of death, suggest that he never quite accepted the truths of the Church. Even his religious poems are wistfully hopeful rather than expectant of heaven. His nuns, priests, and Carthusians believe devoutly in what they serve; but the poet stands always apart from them, admiring, envying, never quite joining. His last word seems to be: "Let us go hence, somewhither strange and cold,/To Hollow Lands . . ." (138).

As for his apparent conversion to the Catholic Church, his friend Victor Plarr writes:

. . . He came to me rather excitedly, and yet shook hands with weak indecision. His hesitating hand-shake, alas! always betrayed a sorrowful fatigue.

"I have been admitted," he said, but he seemed disappointed, for the heavens had not fallen, nor had a sign been vouchsafed. The priest who had admitted him had done so quite casually and had seemed bored. Afterwards, it seemed to me, he forgot all about his religion with surprising alacrity. Only his poetry bears witness to his romantic admiration of a creed which, after all, he shares with many Protestants and Agnostics.[10]

As Plarr suggested, the appeal of the Catholic Church for Dowson was romantic more than religious. But if Dowson the man failed to become a good Catholic, Dowson the poet gained from the association, as four of his poems attest. "Nuns of the Perpetual Adoration" points a contrast, in stately iambic quatrains, between life in a convent and life beyond the walls. To Dowson the convent stands in aloof perfection. The nuns have seen the hollow glories of the world, its bitterness and travail: "Therefore they rather put away desire/And crossed their hands and came to sanctuary. . . ." For reward they gain "serene insight/of the illuminating dawn to be." Through the first seven stanzas he seems to identify himself with the nuns, to see through their eyes and to share their dawn. But a brief identification with believers is as close as he can come to believing. He cannot embrace the dawn in his own separate person, and in the eighth and last stanza, he sadly admits his apartness: "Yea for our roses fade, the world is wild;/But there, beside the altar, there, is rest" (43).

"Benedictio Domini" ("The Blessing of God") treats the same theme in the same meter, but a church rather than a convent becomes the refuge of religion against the world. Images of silence and sound emphasize the contrast. Outside the church are the "sounding street," "sullen noises," and the "hoarse and blaspheming" voice of London. Inside the walls are "bowed heads," "silent blessing," and "strange silence." Here, as in some of his stories, he has muted sounds and blurred colors; he has painted a twilight instead of a dawn or a sunset.

In subject and mood the poem recalls Lionel Johnson's "The Church of a Dream," and it is probable that Dowson, as Johnson's friend, had read the earlier poem before he wrote his own. Both describe misty, incense-laden churches where a single priest—in Dowson, "one old priest"; in Johnson, "one ancient Priest"—performs a ritual. But Dowson's poem is immeasurably superior. Johnson has chosen to write in ponderous hexameters, and to fill out his lines he has stooped to loose, threadbare adjectives like "glorious," "tremulous," and "mystical." A certain dreamlike vagueness befits the subject, but Johnson is more than vague; he is dim and diffuse, and without the incantatory music which justifies the diffuseness of Swinburne. Dowson in his shorter pentameters is spare, firm, and arresting. The air stirs with "the admonition of a silver bell," and the altar is "dressed like a bride, illustrious with light." Plarr once complained that Johnson was a much better Catholic than Dowson: "Johnson, at least, could give chapter and verse for his conversion." But Dowson as a poet is at least a cardinal to Johnson's acolyte.

Like "Benedictio Domini" and "Nuns of the Perpetual Adoration," a third poem, "Carthusians," contrasts the sacred with the secular world. The iambic hexameters, metrically equivalent to but much stronger than those of Johnson in "The

Church of a Dream," depict a Carthusian monastery: "Nothing finds entry here of loud or passionate;/This quiet is the exceeding profit of their pains" (107). Let men like St. Dominic preach holy wrath, says the poet, and men like St. Francis, kindness. In spite of their holiness, they were part of the world; while the Carthusian monks have renounced the world and shall find their reward in heaven. Hopefully Dowson exclaims in the seventh stanza, "Ye shall prevail at last! Surely ye shall prevail!" And yet he implies a doubt: he concludes his poem with the same exclamation, as if, by repeated insistence, to convince both himself and his reader that the hope is also a truth.

However comforting the walls of a convent, a church, or a monastery, there is one flight less assailable, that of Neobule and the "dead child"—death. The faultless octosyllables of "Extreme Unction," a poem dedicated to Lionel Johnson, concern the last rites:

> Upon the eyes, the lips, the feet,
> On all the passages of sense,
> The atoning oil is spread with sweet
> Renewal of lost innocence.

The phrase "all the passages of sense" is taken from *Marius, the Epicurean,* and one critic has suggested that he borrowed his description of the last rites from a scene in *Madame Bovary.*[11] But the final stanzas speak for Dowson himself. As a very young man of twenty-two, he had written "Immortality! Wretched ideal. Infinite ennui—I die at the thought." At the time, he seemed to envision immortality as a continuation of the same brain in the same body. In "Extreme Unction," however, he changes his mind; if there is an afterlife, perhaps it is not a continuation but a sublimation of the flesh:

> Yet, when the walls of flesh grow weak,
> In such an hour, it may well be,
> Through mist and darkness, light will break,
> And each anointed sense will see. (83)

"It may well be"—once again, the hope but not the assurance. Like Christina Rossetti, he desires a better land. Like her, he also seeks escape from a life he does not understand, a life which continuously assaults him with wracking illness and unrequited love. But he differs from her in his view of that better land. At the end of the road which winds uphill, Miss Rossetti knows that there are "beds for all who come." Has she not seen, once in a dream, the flowers "that bud and bloom in Paradise?" But Dowson is far from sure of Paradise. The nearest he can come to certainty is to write about those who, like Christina, are certain.

Dowson was an uncertain Catholic but a good poet. If he could not wholly accept the truths of the Church, her lore and her laws, and her promise of immortality, he nevertheless gave service through his poems. Less confident but no less sincere than Miss Rossetti's "The Road Uphill" and "Paradise," his religious poems deserve a place among the small masterpieces of sacred literature. If they do not speak for a dedicated Catholic, they speak for an eloquent and anguished pagan who, when the temples of Aphrodite crumble in the rain and the altars of Athene lie ungarlanded, approaches the new cathedral and stares timidly through her stained glass windows.

IV *Escape*

Four of Dowson's poems are difficult to classify. Love does not sadden, religion illuminate, nor death darken them; and nature is nowhere in evidence. Except for a preponderance of "to's," the varied titles have nothing in common: "To William Theodore Peters on His Renaissance Cloak," "To One in Bedlam," "The Three Witches," and "To a Lady Asking Foolish Questions." But the poems after all contain a common theme: the poet's wish to escape to other lands and times, or behind barriers in his own land and time. We have met the theme in Dowson's other poems: the wish to escape through death or religion or love: through the grave of Neobule in "A Requiem," the convent walls in "Nuns of the Perpetual Adoration," the wine and roses in "Cynara." In the difficult-to-classify poems, the motive remains unchanged but the means are different.

"To William Theodore Peters on His Renaissance Cloak" hints at a route of escape in its long-winded title. Peters was an actor and producer for whom Dowson wrote his *Pierrot of the Minute*; when he dons his cloak,

> *. . . haply it shall seem,*
> *The curtain of old time is set aside;*
> *As through the sadder coloured throng you gleam;*
> *We see once more fair dame and gallant gay,*
> *The glamour and the grace of yesterday:*
> *The elder, brighter age of pomp and pride.* (120)

The entire nineteenth century, from the Romantics to the Decadents, was a time when poets retreated into the past as readily as H. G. Wells was soon to invade the future. Keats returned to mythical Greece (*Endymion*), Tennyson to Arthurian England (*Idylls of the King*); and Swinburne to the Ireland of Iseult (*Tristram of Lyonesse*) and to the Scotland of Mary Stuart (*Chastelard*). In Dowson's own day Austin Dobson, a poet who shared his liking for the rondeau and the villanelle, haunted the eighteenth century and earlier eras. "When Burbadge played," he sang nostalgically of Shakespeare's friend, the actor Richard Burbadge, as Dowson was to sing of Peters. Dowson himself, as a rule, did not like to linger in history. He preferred to bring Horace and Propertius into the present and turn Lalage into Adelaide. But wooed by the magic of Peters and his Renaissance cloak, he forgot Adelaide long enough to remember Lorenzo and the Borgias, and to sigh for the "glamour and the grace" which he sadly missed in Victoria's industrialized England.

Dowson proposes another and more eccentric escape in "Bedlam." At first it may seem inexplicable that he could envy a man in Bedlam, a place of such riotous horror that it has passed into the language as a synonym for chaos. But the man's blessedness is the fact that the real world does not exist for him. His "delicate mad hands" twist "scentless wisps of straw" into "moon-kissed roses," and his dreams encompass the stars. Dull and pitying men stare at him, but

> *. . . Know they what dreams divine*
> *Lift his long, laughing reveries like enchanted wine,*
> *And makes his melancholy germane to the stars'?* (46)

Far from pitying him, the poet would like to share his dreams, his escape. The man in his bliss resembles the Nuns of the Perpetual Adoration; like the prayerful women, he has found his "illuminating dawn," and Dowson extols and envies him with a fervor which is almost religious.

In "The Three Witches" he proposes a third escape. Though he does not appear in the poem, his choice of subject, witchcraft, is in itself a flight from the everyday world, with its fixed scientific laws; and he makes the witches envison a further flight. Their present situation, it seems, riding the night, has failed to satisfy them. As "dear abortions" of Astarte, the queen of magic and darkness, they yearn for hell:

> *Burning ramparts, ever burning!*
> *To the flame which never dies*
> *We are yearning, yearning, yearning,*
> *With our gay and tearless eyes.* (109)

It is possible that he found his witches in *Macbeth*. On the whole he thought little of Shakespeare, but he must have read the great tragedies at Oxford or earlier and, as a Decadent, could be expected to like the more fantastic passages. His trochaic rhythm, on the other hand, recalls "The Raven" of Poe, his favorite American writer. But subject and rhythm, though possibly derivative, are adapted to his own purpose. Even when he wrote about witches, he could not imagine them happily situated; like him, they wish to escape. As Wilde might have punned, the grass looks grimmer in hell.

"To a Lady Asking Foolish Questions" is a much more explicit poem about escape. In answer to every question the poet reveals his longing:

> *Why am I sorry, Chloe? Because the moon is far:*
> *And who am I to be straightened in a little earthly star?*
>
> *Because thy face is fair? And what if it had not been,*
> *The fairest face of all is the face I have not seen.*
>
> *Because the land is cold, and however I scheme and plot,*
> *I can not find a ferry to the land where I am not.* (130)

In his short and unhappy life, Dowson never found a ferry. Wherever he went—in France or in England—he carried with him his sick body and his grieving heart. Wealthier or healthier, he might have visited his brother Rowland in Canada or re-visited the Italy which he had loved as a child, but he must have guessed that even in foreign lands he could find no "fortunate islands." Only in poems can he ply the seas of escape, and even then his voyage is tinged with sadness. The madman he envies communes with the stars yet partakes of their melancholy. The three witches, though queens of the night, yearn for the fires of hell. So deep is the poet's pessimism that the furthest flight cannot outrun its shadow. But if, as usual, he seems the Charon of poets, ferrying the souls of the dead, for once he is ferrying them away from and not toward hell. That he fails to reach daylight is not a weakness, for the voyage itself is eerily beautiful.

CHAPTER 4

In Praise of Littleness

THE PIERROT OF THE MINUTE, Dowson's only play, is a one-act fantasy in heroic couplets. Written in 1892, produced by William Theodore Peters at the Albert Hall Theatre, and first published in 1897, it has since been set to music by Granville Bantock and acted by little theaters and at American colleges. It is, as critics have noted, a "slight thing," [1] but the adjective should not be used in reproach. The slightness of the play, both in length and subject, is deliberate and justified. As Bernard Muddiman wrote in *The Men of the Nineties*:

... the large canvas, the five-act play, the long novel were démodé for the period. . . . Conder paints small objects like fans and diminutive water-colours and Crackanthorpe writes short stories. The poems of Dowson are short swallow flights of song, and the epic is reduced to Stephen Phillips's *Marpessa.* The one-act play begins on the Continent to make a big appeal for more recognition than that of a curtain-raiser. Small theatres, particularly in Germany and Austria, give evening performances consisting of one-acters alone. It becomes the same in music. The age was short-winded and its art, to borrow a phrase from the palaestra, could only stay over short distances. [2]

In keeping with the trend of the times, Dowson has purposely limited his acts to one, his characters to two, his scene to a park, and his time to a single night. But he has wrought as carefully as a craftsman of Tanagra modeling a terra cotta figurine. If he has not, like that craftsman, lavished many hues on his creation, he has painted so well in silver that few will lament the lack of flesh colors.

The plot is appropriately simple. In the last half of the eighteenth century a young man named Pierrot, once a page but become a courtier, finds a mysterious scroll which directs him to the grove of Cupid near the Petit Trianon at Versailles. He goes to the grove and, in the shadow of a temple to the love god, encounters a daughter of the moon, who promises a night of perfect love that will leave him forever discontented with mortal women. Is he willing to pay such a price for her gift? He accepts. At first they play at love, as Marie Antoinette played at being a shepherdess; but, when day approaches, their love grows wistful and urgent. Dawn breaks. Sadly the Moon Maiden returns Pierrot to his home, asleep, and decrees that he shall remember the night as a dream, "yet still be sorrowful, for a dream's sake."

Classical materials abound not only in the lunar lineage of the heroine and in the presence of a Doric temple to the love god but in countless allusions throughout the play. The grove is said to belong to Venus as well as to Cupid. The maiden dances to a melody made by Pan in Arcady. Her lips are colder than the land of Arctus, god of the frozen north. Pierrot accuses the Fates, Clotho and her sisters, of having involved him in a hopeless love for the maiden. But such materials are altered to the intentions of the poet; diminished to a new framework. The entire play, in fact, is a triumph of diminution.

Significantly the Moon Maiden, though a goddess, is not the actual moon, Diana, Artemis, or Selene, but one of her daughters. Perhaps Dowson feared that the moon herself, who ordered Actaeon's hounds to dismember him because he spied her naked, was too august and Olympian for the little drama he wished to portray. Artemis was not the kind of woman to play in a park with a mortal. Though she sometimes loved men like Endymion and Orion, she never forgot her divinity, her augustness; and her love, one imagines, was awesome and even frightening. Endymion slept while she embraced him and mothered his fifty children; had he stayed awake, he might, like Danaë with Zeus, have been blasted by her splendor. Orion, who joined her in the hunt, was no mere mortal but a powerful giant conditioned to a goddess's company. In short, Artemis was much more suited to Greek tragedy—to a play like Euripides' *Hippolytus*—than to an evening's idyll in a

French park. Dowson's maiden is closer to the goddess in Keats' *Endymion*, who dazzles her mortal lover but does not dismay him. But Dowson has diminished his heroine a further degree. Where the goddess of Keats is vibrant and golden haired, with locks which are "passionately bright," Dowson's is cool and silver and hushed into soft humanity.

Dowson has matched his maiden with a youth of similar qualities. The name "Pierrot" in French means "little Pierre," and the decade which, as Muddiman notes, cultivated littleness, scattered Pierrots through much of its literature. In *Under the Hill* Beardsley speaks of "little Pierrots posing as lady lovers." Symons has a poem called "Pierrot in Half-Mourning," about a lover who hides like a "lost child" when his sweetheart rejects him. Verlaine hails the boy Rimbaud in "Pierrot the Gamin." All of these treatments state or imply smallness: in Beardsley's "little," in Symons' "half-mourning" and "lost child," in Verlaine's "gamin." Though French pantomime shows Pierrot as tall rather than short, he leaves an impression of littleness because he makes light of great passions and pretends that they are trifles. If Pierre is the serious lover whom the ladies take seriously, Pierrot, however tall, becomes his diminutive, to be taken lightly. Dowson's hero falls well within the tradition of littleness. He comes to a glade near the *Petit Trianon* (not the Grand Trianon), finds a *little* statue of Cupid, drinks wine from a *little* basket, and meets the Moon Maiden, who reads to him from a *little* book. All this time one seems to see him, together with his maiden, as a figure in a shadow box, framed and reduced by distance. Hector and Achilles in the *Iliad* seem larger than life; though mortal, they loom like giants because their deeds are gargantuan. Pierrot and the maiden seem smaller than life, with the piquant smallness of sylphs or peris.

To accommodate the hero and heroine, the action of the play is both brief and slight. The time allowed them to love, though literally a whole night, is figuratively a single minute, in other words a moment in the stream of life; and the deeds allowed them are reduced to proportionate size. The goddess in Keats conveys her lover on a reeling tour of heaven, where he meets the Olympians, draws Apollo's bow, and lifts Athene's shield. But Dowson's lovers are much less adventuresome. For

the space of their night they talk, they pretend, they kiss with
the utmost delicacy; and Pierrot describes the flight he would
like to take but never takes. Even his dream of flying is oddly
restrained. He would like to be drawn by a team of "milk-
white butterflies" and not, like Keats' Endymion, borne on a
winged and jet-black steed. In place of lusty Olympians and
the heroic mortals who loved and sometimes battled them, in
place of the less formidable but nevertheless robust goddess
and mortal of Keats, Dowson has given us a pair of exquisite
sylphs engaged in a pantomime.

It does not follow, however, that Dowson has therefore failed
as a poet or as a playwright. There are other virtues besides
power and magnitude. There are figurines as well as monu-
mental sculptures. He has sought and achieved the intimate
rather than the cosmic. He does not attempt to engulf his
reader; only to charm him. When Robinson Jeffers invokes the
figures of Classical mythology—Helen or Clytemnestra, Orestes
or Agamemnon—his verses blaze like a brush fire, crackle and
soar and flourish; he burns us with Jovian passions. To reach
the peace of his "tower beyond tragedy" (that is, of union
with nature), we must first be shattered along with his characters by terror and pity. When Hilda Doolittle resurrects Helen
or Eurydice, she demands of her readers, as well as of her
heroines, a purity burning in its whiteness, a total purging of
human frailties. Dowson in contrast both gives and demands
much less.

His play resembles the paintings of Watteau in which the
mythological figures are pretty and graceful rather than
Olympian. They disport themselves in Fontainebleu, not
Arcadia, and their costumes are the fans and furbelows of
aristocrats instead of the chitons of the Greeks or the tunics
of the Romans. Dowson too has transferred his goddess to a
French setting: she finds her Endymion at Versailles, not on
Mount Latmos; they discuss the gods but also the French
court; and Pierrot teaches her how to speak like a lady of
fashion. Readers of Dowson may think of Watteau's *Les
Champs Élysées,* a diminutive painting of 16⅜ by 12½ inches,
with a similar mood of rococo elegance and a classical statue
to hint that the Olympians have moved to France. Like Watteau and unlike the Greeks, Dowson is decorative rather than

powerful, and again like Watteau, he diminishes the gods instead of enlarging them. But his hero and heroine, in spite of their rococo setting, do not belong to Watteau. Stylized they are but not sophisticated. Though they play at love in a French garden, their kisses are those of children. At heart, Pierrot and his Moon Maiden are neither Greek nor French; they are Dowson himself and his Adelaide grown to womanhood. They wander, it is true, in a foreign garden, but they love with their accustomed innocence.

To express and reveal his lovers, at once mannered and innocent, he has fashioned heroic couplets which glide like Poe's Nicaean bark, "gently o'er a perfumed sea":

> *How merrily the rosy bubbles pass,*
> *Across the amber crystal of the glass.*[3]

or

> *Methinks his eyes, beneath their silver sheaves,*
> *Rest tranquilly like lilies under leaves.* (156)

Such lines, because of their ease, look easy to write, but their smoothness conceals art. It is no small achievement to sustain them through twenty-three pages, or to write them, as Dowson did, in two short weeks. The alliteration, frequent but not as in Swinburne excessive; the end-stopped lines; and the usually perfect rhymes—all contribute to a seemingly effortless flow. To avoid monotony, the couplets are varied by the insertion of lyrics in contrasting meters, as nimble and airy as the lovers who sing them:

> *Love stays a summer night,*
> *Till lights of morning come;*
> *Then takes her wingéd flight*
> *Back to her starry home.* (180)

In the first decades of this century, many poets rejected the polish and smoothness of writers like Dowson in favor of the laconic free verse of the Imagists and the freer, more rugged verse of Carl Sandburg. A few years after Dowson's death, T. E. Hulme, the first real Imagist, wrote:

I walked abroad,
And saw the ruddy moon lean over a hedge
Like a red-faced farmer.[4]

The verse is free, where Dowson's is iambic. Except for the first line, it does not flow: it lumbers, as indeed it should. It is rightly conversational rather than metrical because anything smoother would seem an incongruous vehicle for the earthy image of the moon as a red-faced farmer. Dowson, who saw the moon more conventionally but no less convincingly as a maiden, was also wise in his choice of form. Pierrot and the Moon Maiden would have lost their dreamlike charm if they had talked to each other in free verse. Lines which are suitable to describe a red-faced farmer are not appropriate to be spoken by a white-faced goddess and a young courtier.

If the lines please the ear with their flow, they also please the eye with their softly glittering images. Searchers after sensation, the Decadent poets reveled in images and cataloged flowers and insects, precious stones and even furniture, with the loving pride of a numismatist collecting rare coins. One gem was not enough; there must be a treasure trove. One color seemed to them colorless; there must be kaleidoscopes. Wilde, for example, enumerates gems in *Salomé* until they sing like an incantation: "I have opals that burn always, with an icelike flame, opals that make sad men's minds, and are fearful of the shadows. I have onyxes like the eyeballs of a dead woman. I have moonstones that change when the moon changes, and are wan when they see the sun." [5] Dowson also catalogs, with equal skill but less flamboyance:

> *Hard by a green lagoon our palace rears*
> *Its dome of agate through a myriad years.*
> *A hundred chambers its bright walls enthrone,*
> *Each one carved strangely from a precious stone.*
> *Within the fairest, clad in purity,*
> *Our mother dwelleth immemorially:*
> *Moon-calm, moon-pale, with moon stones on her gown*
> *The floor she treads with little pearls is sown;*
> *She sits upon a throne of amethysts,*
> *And orders mortal fortunes as she lists. . . .* (172)

Thomas Hardy was later to protest the jeweled phrases of the Decadents and other nineteenth-century poets—their adjectives as well as their catalogs—but a present-day reader, after half a century of poets who have vigorously avoided such phrases, may find them refreshing, at least in Dowson. They are rather like the pendants and brooches of earlier centuries. The designs, though dated, continue to please the eye with their polish and color. One is not required to wear them, only to admire. Taken as a whole, in fact, *Pierrot* is a charming museum piece. Since Dowson looked back instead of forward for his inspiration—to Greece and monarchist France instead of to England in the 1890's—he dated his play even while he wrote; and he admittedly wrote with no other purpose than to escape a world which he found oppressive. But Pierrot and his maiden are still good company for dreamers, and their "minute" of summer love has kept its moonlight.

CHAPTER 5

Of Love and Loss

DOWSON WAS above everything a lyric poet; but his stories and sketches and even, at times, his translations, show some of the grace and delicacy which characterize his poems. Unfortunately, the demands of prose are different from those of poetry, and the lyric impulse in Dowson's prose is not always sufficient to transcend his limitations as a story-teller. His prose succeeds in reverse proportion to its length: the longer the piece, the harder it was for the poet to show his hand. The six sketches, on the whole, are much the best; then the eight short stories; and then the nine translations (his two novels, in spite of their mediocrity, deserve a chapter to themselves). Dowson once said of Poe that he was "a master of both prose and verse . . . his prose better than his verse, as mine is." [1] Such a categorical statement, while true of Poe, must be amended for Dowson. On the contrary, his verse is better than his prose, which succeeds only when it approaches verse.

I *The Sketches*

Mark Longaker writes of Dowson's sketches (which, with one exception, appeared in *Decorations*): "It was in the pieces in which he was not burdened by the necessity of telling a sustained story that Dowson did his finest work in prose. 'The Dying of Francis Donne,' 'Absinthia Taetra,' and 'The Visit' are unmistakably poetic." [2] The stories, we will see, suffer from pallid characterization and monotony of plot; but their flashes of poetry somewhat redeem them. The sketches on the other hand, most of them a page or less in length, do not pretend to tell a story or to present three-dimensional characters; hence, they arouse no large expectations. Promising less than the stories, they give much more. Three of them deal with the poison of disillusionment; three, with antidotes.

The three sketches which deal with disillusionment were published in 1899, two years after Adelaide Foltinowicz's marriage to her father's waiter. The marriage convinced Dowson that his princess of dreams was, after all, fallible. Perhaps the first two sketches and certainly the third reflect his bitter disappointment. In "The Fortunate Islands" the speaker questions a group of bearded mariners who have come from perilous voyages. He tells them about the woman he has searched for, the ideal friend, the perfect country. Do these things truly exist? "Each raised a hand of asseveration; and they said: 'We tell you the truth: there are no fortunate islands'" (148). In "Market" a man greets a maiden on her way to town. He lists the delicacies she might be carrying to market, "little pats of yellow butter, new-laid eggs, this morning's mushrooms . . ." (149). Instead she is empty-handed. When he asks the reason, the coquetry of her answer hints that she intends to peddle herself. In "The Princess of Dreams" a knight approaches a castle to liberate a waiting princess. Unlike the dilatory hero of Christina Rossetti's "The Prince's Progress" (a poem which Dowson admired), he arrives in good time. But he finds that his princess' tower "is not of ivory and that she is not even virtuous nor a princess" (152).

Such disillusionments demand antidotes, which Dowson has supplied in three additional sketches. "Absinthia Taetra," recalling De Quincey's *Confessions of an Opium-Eater*, invokes the forgetfulness of absinthe. The sketch is distinguished by two kinds of imagery, both much prized by the Decadents with their love for exoticism: jewels and savage beasts. When mixed with water, the speaker tells us, absinthe changes color, flows from emerald to opal, and offers oblivion from past, present, and future. "The past tore after him like a panther and through the blackness of the present he saw the luminous tiger eyes of things to be." He drinks opaline and for a little while forgets, but nothing is changed—the "tiger menace" is still "red in the sky" (150). An escape more permanent is needed.

In "The Visit" he confronts such escape in the form of a visitor:

But all my wonder was gone when I looked again into the eyes of my guest, and I said:
"I have wanted you all my life."
Then said Death (and what reproachful tenderness was shadowed in his obscure smile):
"You had only to call." (151)

The death wish prevalent in the poems here receives its most unequivocal expression. Death, far from being a madman with a scythe, is a bringer of peace. Though physically he is not described except in his "supreme and sorrowful smile," he suggests the winged god Thanatos whom the artist Oswyn paints in *A Comedy of Masks,* the beautiful boy who comes with a rustle of wings and with hands as cool as myrrh—a reliever, not a destroyer.

A fuller treatment of death appears in "The Dying of Francis Donne," which because of its length—eleven pages—is sometimes called a short story, though it lacks both conflict and detailed characterization. At thirty-five a famous English doctor learns that he is going to die of an incurable disease. He withdraws to a small village in France, because he prefers to die as "a stranger in a strange land." When death comes, "All that was distorted in life was adjusted and justified in the light of his sudden knowledge" (147). It is Dowson's own story, of course, that of the still young man aware that he is doomed, dreading and yet somehow craving the end. It is also a timeless story, which takes for its epigraph a line from Genesis, "Dust thou art and to dust returnest," and which quotes the passage from I Corinthians ending, "O death, where is thy sting?" and also the Emperor Hadrian's famous address to his soul. Hebrew and Roman, the quotations seem to say, await the Englishman in the same oblivious dust. "The Dying of Francis Donne" is perhaps the most famous of all Dowson's prose. First published in *The Savoy* and reprinted in Edward J. O'Brien's *Great Modern English Stories* (1919), it has been called "not only a penetrating study in the psychology of the contemplation of death, but a searching revelation of Dowson's attitude as well" (158).

The power of the sketches, which resemble without echoing the prose poems of Baudelaire, is that of the best poetry—compression, rhythmical language, and provocative images. Had Dowson lived a little later, he might have written free verse instead of prose poems. "Absinthia Taetra," especially, if broken into irregular lines, would make an excellent Imagist poem. Its shifting colors and its tiger eyes anticipate Amy Lowell with her "tiger sun" and her "Leopard eyes of marigolds crouching above red earth." In short, the sketches have the virtues of Dowson's stories: their elegiac poetry, without their liabilities. In all of his work, only his best poems surpass them.

II *The Short Stories*

Dowson's short stories, all of which appeared first in magazines and five of which were collected in a volume called *Dilemmas* (1895), have a common theme: the loss of love. With one exception ("The Diary of a Successful Man") love is lost not through fate or ironic coincidence as in Hardy, but through the deliberate choice of the characters. "There are some renunciations which are better than happiness" (136), remarks Countess Marie of the Angels; and the other characters, tacitly or openly, agree. The loss of love appears in various guises. Much the most frequent is a mature man's loss of a young girl, reflecting, no doubt, the poet's relationship with Adelaide. As we have seen, the same theme unifies his poems. Typically the man is in his thirties, perhaps forty. The years have burdened and embittered him, and he seeks refuge in the love of a young, inexperienced girl like the following: "She was very young and slight—she might have been sixteen—and she had a singularly pretty face; her white dress was very simple, and her little straw hat, but both of these she wore with an air which at once set her apart from her companions, with their provincial finery and their rather commonplace charms" (92-93). Young, slight, virginal, and artless in manner and dress: this, to Dowson's heroes, is the ideal; and her growing up is a growing away from perfection, since mature women, whatever their virtues, have lost the pristine freshness of girlhood. Whenever possible, his heroes resist or evade the inevitable growth of their paragons.

In "The Statute of Limitations" the Englishman Michael Garth, too poor to marry the girl of his choice, sails to Peru in search of a fortune. His sweetheart has promised to wait for his return. After several years she sends him a picture of herself: "A beautiful face still but certainly the face of a woman, who had passed from the grace of girlhood . . . to a dignity touched with sadness: a face, upon which life had already written some of its cruelties" (87). Resenting the change, he lingers in Peru for twelve years, long after he has amassed a fortune. At last, and with great reluctance, he sails for home, but during the voyage he drowns himself in the ocean.

In "Apple Blossom in Brittany" the Englishman Benedict Campion is the guardian of the French girl, Marie-Ursule. Desperately in love with her but many years her senior (he is forty, she sixteen), he hesitates to propose marriage. He fears that he will taint her innocence and watch her cheapen before his eyes. When she asks his permission to become a nun, he knows that he has only to offer marriage and that she will prefer him to the Church. But the Church will preserve her innocence, insulate her from the contaminating world: "He felt at once and finally, that he acquiesced in it; that any other ending to his love had been an impossible grossness, and that to lose her in just that fashion was the only way in which he could keep her always" (106).

In "A Case of Conscience," another Englishman, Sebastian Murch, also mature in years, with lines of lassitude around his mouth and the "air of having tasted widely," falls in love with a young French girl, Marie-Yvonne, and wishes to marry her. But his best friend reminds him that he has been married previously; Marie-Yvonne, as a good Catholic, will doubtless refuse to marry a divorced man. Shall he tell her his secret and lose her love? At the end of the story his decision to confess is implied if not stated: ". . . then she turned, to recognize the long stooping figure of Sebastian Murch, who advanced to meet her" (82).

Sometimes the lovers are closer to the same age, but no more successful at getting together. In "The Eyes of Pride" the artist Seefang and the worldly Rosalind reject each other, despite a powerful mutual attraction, because of their proud temperaments and fierce angers. In "The Diary of a Successful Man" two friends propose to the same woman at the same time. She writes to each of them, rejecting one and accepting the other, but confuses her notes; and for twenty-five years the hero is unaware that it was he and not his friend she had meant to choose. By then she has long since become a nun, and he has married a commonplace woman and gained worldly success without happiness. In "Countess Marie of the Angels," Colonel Mallory hears about the unsuccessful marriage of an old sweetheart, Marie, and offers his love. She refuses him because her husband, though separated from her, is still alive. Later the husband dies and she refuses the Colonel again because, in the Colonel's words, "There is a season for all things, for one's happiness as for the rest, and missing it once, one misses it forever . . ." (135).

Sometimes the lost love is platonic rather than romantic. In "An Orchestral Violin" a gifted singer dismisses the music teacher who has been like a father to her when he opposes her marriage to a scoundrel. The marriage fails but the singer and the teacher, for unexplained reasons, are never reconciled. In "Souvenirs of an Egotist," Dowson's first published story, a famous musician listens to a barrel organ and remembers how, in his boyhood, he rejected the only person he ever loved, a girl in the Paris gutters who, when he faced starvation, became a sister to him and bought him his first violin.

The loss of love, which confronts us daily, is a rich and durable theme for short stories; but when eight stories, however different in setting, all concern characters who lose love, and when most of these characters invite the loss rather than having it thrust upon them, then the bias of the writer is evident. Even in the story in which the loss is an accident, "The Diary of a Successful Man," the confusion of notes seems deliberately contrived: it is as if Dowson is saying that people are doomed to bring loss on themselves, if not consciously then accidentally. He does, at least, allow various consolations to his characters: one man becomes a famous musician; another makes a fortune in Peru; another appeases his conscience. But the consolation rarely seems worth the renunciation. The plain fact is that most of the characters are afraid to participate in life. They would rather withdraw from love, regardless of the consequences, than embrace it and risk being hurt or disillusioned.

Henry James, no doubt, is partly to blame for the passiveness of Dowson's characters. James, his favorite American novelist, excelled at creating men who avoid action, who deliberate instead of do and then persuade themselves that they have followed the right course. But Dowson's own character, conditioned by the events of his life, is a much more significant factor. During his last decade sickness enervated him and the tragic deaths of both of his parents in the same year shattered him. He sought refuge in absinthe and in other dissipations which gave him temporary relief but undermined his health. It is not surprising that the same theme pervades his poems, his play, and his stories: life at best is joyless, pleasures are brief, death ends everything. As he wrote in "Sapientia Lunae":

> *The wisdom of the world said unto me:*
> "Go forth and run, the race is to the brave;
> Perchance some honour tarrieth for thee!"
> *"As tarrieth," I said, "for sure, the grave."*[3]

Confronted with such "wisdom," he wandered, delayed, and dreamed. He procrastinated in his courtship of Adelaide and lost her to another man. He vacillated in his writing until Arthur Moore had to finish *Adrian Rome*. His heroes are himself; they mirror in prose the indecisiveness of his own life. They would rather renounce than participate. Behind them, however, one perceives not a shallow man, but one too sensitive for his own good. He feels so much and so deeply that even on the printed page he must limit experience until it becomes endurable.

The limitations of Dowson's method are severe. His pattern of love and loss is bound to grow monotonous, when every conflict is resolved by withdrawal. Nor does he compensate for weak plotting by the range and power of his characters. Most of his men, as we have seen, are Dowson himself; most of his women are the type of the innocent girl he believed he had found in Adelaide. The heroines who depart from this type—the haughty Madame Romanoff in "An Orchestral Violin" and the proud Rosalind in "The Eyes of Pride"—are

welcome for the sake of variety but they are much less convincing. In painting scene, he is more successful though hardly
exceptional. Longaker writes of "The Diary of a Successful
Man": "There is little in the story . . . which shows a penetrating observation of Flemish local colour" (155). The same
can be said of the other stories and other backgrounds, and
even Iquique, Peru, which offered a fresh and piquant subject
in "The Statute of Limitations," is indistinguishable from a
thousand other towns in South American countries. If he did
not choose to visualize his scenes through realistic details, he
might have borrowed the method of Poe and substituted a
cloudy but alluring exoticism; or borrowed from his own poems
the bizarre Latin names, the mist, and the shadows. But
strangeness too is lacking.

What remains is a single excellence which compensates for
many limitations. The stories in their best moments approach
poetry. The sentences are chiseled and balanced without being
heavily formal; their length is varied to suit the substance and
also to please the ear. An almost funereal music beats behind
the words. While the scenes as a whole are bare, isolated
images throb and burn with color: blood-red sarrazin glints
in the reader's eye, a lichened church spire lingers in his mind.
At times even the dialogue sings, though written in the ca-
dences of conversation: " 'But the blossom is so much prettier,'
she protested; 'and there will be apples and apples—always
enough apples. But I like the blossom best—and it is so soon
over' " (104). Elegies written in prose, the stories make life
musical if not meaningful. Dowson's heroes love and lose and
grow no wiser, and his heroines climb to the compromise which
is womanhood and decline to the ruin which is age. He offers
them to us neither as examples to follow nor to avoid; he
simply records their sighs. But the sighs are exquisite. His quiet
dreamers are far from the multicolored human comedy of
Balzac and as far from the robust Realism of Zola, writers he
admired and translated into English; but literature needs its
twilights as well as its mornings and afternoons.

III   *The Translations*

Dowson was a poet and novelist by inclination and a translator because he needed to earn a living. He made little

through the sale of his richly bound but poorly selling books, and very little more through the poems and stories he sold to magazines. For a time his father helped to support him with profits from his dock in Limehouse, but the dock, already out of date when inherited by Alfred Dowson, fell into disrepair and had to be leased and finally sold. Beginning in 1893, Dowson undertook a number of translations to provide himself with a source of income.

His first translation, sponsored by the Lutetian Society, was Zola's *La Terre,* which brought him a fee of fifty pounds. For a number of reasons the task was irksome to him. Zola at the time was considered a little scandalous by most Englishmen, and a previous translator of *La Terre,* Henry Vizetelly, had spent six months in jail. In the words of Victor Plarr, Dowson was hard pressed to "render certain Rabelaisian phrases into something less offensive in English—into common cleanly blasphemies at least." [4] This problem, and the fact that he did not like the enforced discipline of sustained translation, led him to complain to Plarr that he was "overwhelmed" by Zola. He had to be prodded by his editor to finish the project.

In spite of his troubles with *La Terre,* however, he soon joined Teixeira de Mattos in a translation of Couperus' *Majesty;* and he later translated, alone or with others, such various works as Richard Muther's *The History of Modern Painting,* Balzac's *La Fille aux Yeux d'Or,* Voltaire's *La Pucelle d'Orléans,* Choderlos de Laclos' *Les Liaisons Dangereuses,* Dubois' *Memoirs,* the Goncourt brothers' *The Confidantes of a King,* the fairy tale "Beauty and the Beast," and, in addition to the nine prose translations, a number of poems by Verlaine. Eventually Leonard Smithers agreed to pay him thirty shillings a week for all the material he could translate.

Dowson's range of French, though limited, was sufficient for reasonable accuracy, and the fastidious ear which delighted in the letter "v" and the dreamlike rhythms of Poe assured both grace and polish. But even his contemporaries recognized that a gifted lyric poet was wasting his talent. In many cases vitality as well as lyricism was needed, and Dowson, whatever his virtues, was anything but vigorous. Plarr complained that *La Terre* was forced work and that *The Girl with the Golden Eyes* suffered the same fault. Frank Harris tells of meeting Dowson in a bar off Leicester Square and of hearing him recite a translation from Verlaine. Harris remarked that, though he had caught Verlaine's "ineffable sadness," the translation on the whole was rather poor. " 'So was the price paid for it,' Dowson laughed, 'a measly ten shillings. What can you expect for that?' " [5]

Today his translations, no longer on sale for a guinea in booksellers' windows, are of little interest except for the light they cast on the writers whom he liked to read and who influenced his original work (for he usually chose to translate the writers he admired). If the hours he spent translating "Beauty and the Beast" inspired him to a poem, a sketch, or a story of his own, they were not entirely misspent; few will deny, however, that for purposes of literature, as opposed to the pocketbook, they might have been better spent.

CHAPTER 6

The Misplaced Poet

THE LYRIC poet is a worker in miniature. Moments, not days or weeks, moods, not movement and conflict, provide his materials. Stanzas instead of chapters are his largest units, and his words, being few, cannot be wasted. Like a Swiss toy-maker, he must work with patience and infinite precision. Just as the toymaker may tire of marionettes and long to build manikins or robots, so the lyric poet may aspire to write plays or novels. Shelley wrote verse dramas and Tennyson an Arthurian epic; Swinburne wrote Classical tragedies and a pair of neglected novels; and Ernest Dowson, in addition to writing *The Pierrot of the Minute,* collaborated on two novels, *A Comedy of Masks* and *Adrian Rome.*

The poet accustomed to the narrow dimensions of the sonnet or of the villanelle may suppose that the larger forms offer unlimited freedom. But the novel, though demanding less precision than the lyric, imposes restrictions of a different kind. At the very least, it demands characters who engage our attention and a conflict which sustains our interest. A single mood is sufficient for a lyric; a novel must progress from mood to mood, scene to scene; it must build, disclose, develop. Dowson's own contemporaries recognized that he was a better poet than a novelist. Bernard Muddiman, who thought his best poems immortal, confessed to a lower estimate of his novels: "George Moore wrote a masterpiece in *Evelyn Innes,* but Ernest Dowson and Arthur Moore in *A Comedy of Masks* and *Adrian Rome* did not retaliate." [1] The perspective of years has made it possible to speak with greater bluntness: Dowson was a gifted poet who strayed into writing dull novels.

I A Comedy of Masks

Dowson's collaborator on both of his novels was Arthur Moore, a young man with whom he had shared at Oxford a love for Henry James and with whom he had later taken a walking tour through Brittany. In Brittany they had talked over plans for their first novel, *A Comedy of Masks,* which they began writing in 1892 and finished the next year. Originally called *Masquerade,* the book was rejected by the publisher Bentley; retitled *A Comedy of Masks* at the suggestion of Lionel Johnson, it won acceptance from William Heinemann. Dowson wrote to his friend Plarr just before its publication: "*The Comedy of Masks* appears on Friday. . . . I tremble at the prospect of being reviewed—I am painfully conscious of the innumerable blemishes and alas! the weakest points are in the first volume so that I fear sleep will overcome the reviewer before he reach any of our less banal passages. What fools we are to write—or rather to publish! Mercifully Lionel does not review novels, and as to the opinion of the average novel-reviewing Gallienish animal [a reference to Richard LeGallienne]—we will not think of it." [2] While the book brought him little in royalties or acclaim, it did receive a favorable review in *Bookman,* and he felt encouraged enough to plan a second book with Moore, *Adrian Rome.*

A letter which Moore wrote to Mark Longaker in 1939 explains the manner in which the friends collaborated: "Our first step was to prepare a brief synopsis. . . . This was of a very sketchy kind, and did little more than indicate the more important of the dramatis personae and their general line of conduct. On this foundation, we proceeded to construct the work by each alternately contributing a chapter (or occasionally two). Each installment, as completed in draft, was submitted by the author to his collaborator, so that he might read, criticize, and 'carry on.'" He goes on to say that Dowson wrote the first chapter in *A Comedy of Masks* and he the first in *Adrian Rome,* but the later chapters he now has difficulty in ascribing to either of them. Because of their mutual love for Henry James and other writers, their styles were almost identical.[3]

The plot of *A Comedy of Masks* is slight for three volumes

which together total more than six hundred pages. Rainham, the consumptive owner of a dilapidated dock, befriends Lightmark, a struggling painter, and introduces him to the wealthy and marriageable Eve. When Lightmark marries Eve, Rainham gives his reluctant blessing, though secretly he loves her himself. But then he learns that his supposed friend is really a blackguard who has stolen the idea for his best picture from the much more talented painter, Oswyn. What is more, Lightmark has ruined a model named Kitty and fathered her child. When Kitty accuses her seducer in the presence of his wife, Rainham intercedes and insists that it is he who has ruined the girl, not Lightmark; he thereby spares Eve disillusionment with her husband. On his deathbed, however, he confesses his innocence to Oswyn, who later reveals the truth to Eve. Gallantly (or foolishly) she decides to continue the comedy of masks as the wife of a seducer and thief.

The theme which these characters illustrate with their involvements and confusions is the old, familiar one that all the world is a stage where men and women conceal their tragic feelings behind their comic masks. Rainham says: "Aren't we always being told that life is only a play?" [4] Of Mary, a minor character, it is said that her eyes "had seen through the philosophic indifference of Lady Garnett's shrug, the gentle irony of Rainham's perpetual smile, the various masks of tragic comedians on a stage where there is no prompter, where the footlights are most pitiless, and where the gallery is only too lavish of its cat-calls at the smallest slip" (I, 79). And Oswyn remarks in the last scene: "Go back to your guests; I know, you see, whence you come; take up your part in the play, the masque; be ready with your cues. It's all masks and dominoes; what does the form or colour of it matter? Underneath it all you are yourself, with your beautiful sorrow, your memories, your transcendent happiness—nothing can touch that; what does it matter?" (III, 200).

In illustrating their theme, the authors resemble at times their model, James. They people their pages with sharp-tongued dowagers and pliant, marriageable daughters, dedicated artists and smooth-tongued poseurs; and they conduct them through English drawing rooms and Continental watering places. But they lack James' mastery of language. Their writing is competent, no more. Unlike James, they content themselves with the adequate, not the inevitable word; and their use of French phrases, though accurate enough, seems pedantic instead of right—an annoying display of knowledge rather than an acceptable facet of their style. Their sentences are as neatly built as a brick schoolhouse and no more exciting. James' sentences, in contrast, are built like a Gothic cathedral, with verbal naves and altars, towers which probe the sky, and flying buttresses which, far from superfluous, anchor the heavenly edifice to the earth.

Furthermore, they lack James' ironic insights into the weaknesses of society. They have tried very hard to show a brilliant yet hollow circle, "cultivated, very subtle, very cynical. Their talk, which flashed quickest around Lady Garnett, who was the readiest of them all, could not possibly have been better; it was like the rapid passes of exquisite fencers with foils" (III, 79). Such a statement, however, should be followed by illustration: the talk should be *shown* to flash like the passes of fencers. Lady Garnett and her friends should scintillate and yet at the same time reveal themselves in their hollowness and cynicism. In actual fact, they talk with no more brilliance and no more self-revelation than a table of bridge players who mix bidding and gossip in equal portions.

It is not necessary, of course, that Dowson and Moore should approximate the subtle irony of James. There is also the weapon of satire. In the next decade Edith Wharton was to satirize wealthy Americans in *The House of Mirth* and in *The Age of Innocence*. With a single sentence she can devastate folly and pretension. Of a couple going to church, she remarks: "Mr. and Mrs. Wetherall's circle was so large that God was included in their visiting-list." [5] The lighter approach of Wilde is also possible: "Modern women find a new scandal as becoming as a new bonnet, and air them both in the Park every afternoon." [6] Such people as Dowson and Moore describe, engaged as they are in their comedy of masks, obviously deserve censure; the authors say as much but lack the proper, the deadly weapons with which to assault them: the irony of James or the satire of Wharton and Wilde.

Not all of *A Comedy of Masks* concerns society. There are also scenes in Bohemia. Of Rainham it is said: "Indeed, to

Philip Rainham, who had doubtless in his blood the taint of Bohemia, Brodonowski's and the enthusiasm of its guests had a very definite charm" (I, 51). When Rainham goes to drink at Brodonowski's, he meets his friend Oswyn and others who are meant to typify the artist in his natural habitat. Here was a chance for Dowson to paint from experience, to record the bawdy, witty, and sad conversations he had heard; the turns of phrase, the intonations which localize a scene in one particular city in one particular bar; to describe the bearded men who discuss art and mistresses with equal fervor, and the women who love and listen to them. Here was his opportunity to portray the life which he obviously preferred to the society he condemns in the novel. But the conversations he records are no more flavorful than the talk of tourists who have gone slumming among beatniks. Intoxication, both of art and of alcohol, is missing. As for Oswyn himself, the most Bohemian of artists, he is called unkempt; and late in the story Eve glimpses the dishevelment of his apartment. But the man's soul, no doubt intended to be as disheveled as his clothes and his rooms, and as free from the dictates of society, is hardly intimated. The authors imply a rugged grandeur about him, compounded equally of coarseness and honesty. But they fail to show such qualities with convincing detail.

Dowson himself, carousing from pub to pub with Dulcie on his arm, reciting "Cynara" in a smoky room or scribbling immortal lines on a tabletop, had seen enough of Bohemia to enrich a score of novels, but the reticence which made him give Latin names to modern ladies also constrained him to paint (or allow his collaborator to paint) Bohemia and her natives with a decorous and disappointing vagueness. In his poems the reticence is an asset; by avoiding the contemporary, he gains timelessness. But a novel, by its very nature, promises to grip us with present action and immediate sensations and, failing, fails to live. Had Dowson vividly visualized his scenes of Bohemia and the character of Oswyn instead of glimpsing them, had he spoken from experience as Wilde did in *The Picture of Dorian Gray*, he would greatly have strengthened his book by showing that masks need not always be worn, or if they must, at least there are masks less deceitful than those worn in society—those of the true artist.

[94]

This repeated failure to make the best of materials, whether scenes or characters, is not the only weakness in the book. There is also a sin of excess. Though the plot on the whole is developed with reasonable plausibility, the scene in which Kitty appears on the docks, carrying her illegitimate child and searching for its father, is an unmistakable dash of Victorian melodrama. Indeed, throughout the book both Kitty and her seducer Lightmark function as stereotypes, and the reader is not surprised when Kitty turns her face to the wall and dies in the long-accepted fashion of fallen women.

Though the faults of the book are several, there is a redeeming virtue—the light which it casts on Dowson, the man. The dock described is the one which belonged to his father and which he himself once helped to manage. More important, both Rainham and Oswyn incorporate elements of his own life and character. Rainham shares Dowson's love for childhood: "Children always recognized an ally in the man who made so few friends among his peers, and for children—especially for pretty children of a prettiness which accorded with his own private views—Rainham had an undeniable weakness" (II, 186-87). He also shares Dowson's inertia, his dread of positive action. He loves a girl like Adelaide but allows Lightmark to marry her: "Certainly his vain desire for her personal presence, for the consolation of her voice and eyes, was with him always, like the ache of physical hunger or thirst—the one thing real in a world of shadows" (III, 45). And he dies of consumption, the disease which afflicted the poet, as well as his parents and his brother Rowland.

Oswyn in part is also Dowson, especially in his death wish. To the dying Rainham he says: "It *is* you who are fortunate; you are so nearly done with it all; you've such a long rest before you" (III, 69). His finest achievement is a painting of the Greek death god, Thanatos, the Peacebearer, "pale, with beautiful and wonderfully colored poppies" (III, 109). Again Oswyn reveals Dowson in his contention that the true artist must ignore the demands of society and remain faithful to his own artistic instinct, even if the price is rejection and poverty. But a novel, in order to succeed, must offer more than autobiographical fragments. To the reader acquainted with Dowson's life, such fragments are tantalizing but hardly frequent enough to sustain a weak story. To the reader ignorant of the author's life, they pass unnoticed in the general tedium.

It is not difficult to account for the failure of *A Comedy of Masks*. When two authors collaborate, they are apt to achieve a common denominator. In adapting their styles to each other, they lose, too often, their individuality—the excellence and even the eccentricities which distinguish a good novelist from his contemporaries. The result, while it usually avoids shocking lapses in taste or art, seldom exceeds mere competence. A middle ground, if it lacks deep pits, also lacks mountains. Charles Dickens and Wilkie Collins collaborated on several stories, but each is remembered for the books and stories he wrote by himself. The great collaborators are not those who write alternate chapters in a book but who contribute separate but complementary art forms—Gilbert the lyrics, Sullivan the music, not Gilbert and Sullivan both writing lyrics and both writing music for the same operetta.

But collaboration is not the only or even the main explanation for the failure of *A Comedy of Masks*. Writing alone, Dowson would probably still have failed (even had he managed to complete such a lengthy project without help). The toymaker who attempts to build a robot may find himself baffled by sheer size. The materials with which he must work are strange to him, gross and heavy; and it is not surprising if he uses them without discrimination and, once having used them, fails to recognize his failure. In the same way the lyric poet may flounder in a torrent of words and yet persuade himself, as Dowson did, that his prose is better than his poetry. It is hard to read *A Comedy of Masks* without remembering Wilde's remark: "Anybody can write a three-volume novel. It merely requires a complete ignorance of both life and literature." [7] Though Dowson and Moore were not ignorant of life and certainly not of literature, life inspired them to bottle old wine, soured instead of mellowed, in colorless bottles; and literature gave them a model whom they imitated but woefully failed to equal.

II   Adrian Rome

It is easy to make allowances for a first novel, to excuse a writer's faults by attributing them to inexperience and to find promise when there is not actual achievement. Admirers of Dowson, reading *A Comedy of Masks,* could remind themselves that he was a very young man with no previous novels to his credit, a poet attempting a new form. And they could point out that, while the book was dull, it was not altogether hopeless. But *Adrian Rome* confirms what *A Comedy of Masks* suggests: Dowson is laboring in the wrong field. There is no sign of maturing abilities. The style is neither better nor worse; it remains merely adequate. The characters, for the most part, are as shallowly conceived as Lightmark and Kitty, Rainham and Oswyn; and the conflict in which they engage is no more gripping than a game of shuffleboard. Furthermore, it is hard to find traces of Dowson, the man, which interest the reader as biography even if not as fiction. All in all, *Adrian Rome* represents a slight reversal rather than an improvement.

Perhaps the circumstances of composition are partly to blame. As Moore wrote Longaker:

In the case of our first published novel (*A Comedy of Masks*) we had fairly frequent opportunities for meeting and discussion. This was unfortunately not so in the case of *Adrian Rome,* the greater part of which was written after Dowson had left England to take up his abode in France, where I was not able to join him except for brief periods during my summer holidays. This interruption occurred between the dates of publication of the two novels. Dowson became increasingly more erratic and dilatory as a correspondent, and it became more and more difficult to extract his "copy" from him; indeed, in the end, I found myself compelled to write the last few chapters of *Adrian Rome* without his cooperation.[8]

But authors cannot be excused on the grounds that circumstances were unfavorable to their project. The art of successful writing is learning to transcend difficulties, and the difficulty of collaborating from a distance is one of the numerous obstacles which writers must expect to face and conquer.

The plot can be briefly told. Adrian Rome, a young aristocrat just down from Oxford, seems blessed by the gods: he has already shown promise as a poet, and he loves Sylvia Drew, a virginal young girl with whom he has grown up and who shyly returns his love. Then he makes his mistake. He hesitates to press his suit with her and she, self-conscious because of her modest circumstances, withdraws from his life. Dejected, he gravitates toward London society and, encouraged by the matchmaking Mrs. Vesper, contracts a fashionable marriage with a beauty named Marion Brabant. But Marion is hostile to his art, and her friends and pastimes stultify him. His powers dwindle; he accomplishes little. He recognizes his mistake but does not know how to extricate himself—until he rediscovers Sylvia. She has become a third-rate actress in a neighborhood theater, but her beauty and innocence remain untarnished. In a desperate letter he begs her to sail to the Mediterranean with him on his yacht. At first she refuses; then she reconsiders. At least she should meet him again to say good-bye, she reasons, and she hurries to the appointed rendezvous. She is too late. Adrian has drowned in a fortuitous boating accident.

As the summary indicates, the novel has a theme: the conflict of an artist with society. Shall he do what others expect of him or lead his own life and thereby fulfill his gifts? Writers before and after Dowson, notably James Joyce in *A Portrait of the Artist as a Young Man,* have tried to answer the question. Even today, when dedicated artists still face the same decision, the theme remains valid in the right hands. In *Adrian Rome* it is stated often and clearly. Before Rome has contracted his ill-advised marriage, his artistic ideals are high (and somewhat reminiscent of Pater's aesthetic manifesto): "To be concerned with high passions, to live as fully and intensely as one could, rather than as long and as peacefully as one might,—it seemed to him that it was only under such conditions that the born artist could properly work out his salvation. The fulness of one's life, the fineness of one's impressions, the multiplicity of one's sensations, here it seemed to him was the rough material out of which grew magnificently the ultimate achievement of one's art." [9]

But after Adrian's marriage his one-time guardian remarks with humorous intonation and serious intent: "After all, you disappoint me. . . . You've settled down so promptly—and so well. You've done everything that you ought to do, and left undone all that you shouldn't do. In short, you're unimpeachable correctness" (262). But Adrian and his artistic integrity are not beyond saving: "And then an illumination had come to him, and a sense that a man's folly should not be final; that if one had been imposed upon, even if one had oneself largely contributed to the imposition, one had nevertheless the right to set oneself free, to begin again" (330).

The theme could hardly be stated more plainly. But it is not enough for a novelist to state or to make his characters state a theme, just as it was not enough in *A Comedy of Masks* to call the conversation of Lady Garnett and her circle brilliant without illustrating its brilliance. A novelist must dramatize theme through actions. In life, wisdom is seldom learned except through experience; and novels which seek to illuminate life should present appropriate experience. Mere statement of truth, without accompanying action, threatens to become a sermon. *Adrian Rome* is more than a sermon; there is some attempt to dramatize.

But the great, the unforgivable weakness is that, through most of the book, Adrian is a bore and a boor; and the truth he is meant to express, though always evident, is no more compelling than the man. He is little better company than his frigid wife or the matchmaking Mrs. Vesper or a minor nuisance named Miss Lancaster, who marries for money just as Adrian marries for suitability. For one thing we are never made to believe in his talent as a writer, even before his marriage. He is said to have written a volume of excellent lyrics and a hit play, but the dullness and lethargy of his character, as the authors show him to us, suggest a man without real talent or perception. Furthermore, he is so self-centered that it is hard to sympathize with his plight. He hardly seems worth the saving. Mrs. Vesper indeed encouraged his marriage, but Adrian himself made the choice, and his accusation of the woman is inexcusable: "'You have every right to interfere in my married life.' He let his great bitterness pierce through his calm. 'Didn't you make it?'" (322). When his boat overturns and drowns him, one feels that the authors expect to evoke sympathy. Instead they evoke indifference. Adrian, in spite of his wise decision to run away with Sylvia, is not sympathetic at any time in the novel; he is not even glamorously wicked like Iago and Richard III, who fascinate us with their villainies and whose well-deserved falls enable us to salve our conscience after secretly enjoying their machinations. In a word, the theme of the novel fails to find adequate expression through the misadventures of a dullard.

Like *A Comedy of Masks, Adrian Rome* does have rewarding moments. Gerald Brooke, an Oxford friend of Adrian, typifies the Decadent of the 1890's, and through him Dowson pokes fun at the very group to which he himself belonged. The sprightliest dialogue belongs to Brooke. After a trip to Oxford to pay some bills, he remarks to Adrian:

"For my part, I never go away on the most commonplace errand, but I invent some beautiful, romantic account of myself, for the benefit of my friends. Today I have been picking cowslips on the Cumnor hills."

Adrian smiled.

"Cowslips—in August? My dear Brooke!" he protested.

The other waved his hand with a gesture of benignant tolerance.

"Don't they flourish now? How wonderful of you to know, Adrian! I know nothing about them, except that they rhyme perfectly with 'lips'. . . ." (171-72)

But Brooke is a minor character and the scenes he brightens are few.

In *The Barretts of Wimpole Street* Elizabeth Barrett and Robert Browning agree that they prefer colossal failures to small successes. Dowson's and Moore's novels are failures but, alas, not colossal. They lack even the distinction of being outrageously bad. They commit no blunders which might in their way be engaging, like the ludicrous scene in *Jane Eyre* when Rochester passes himself off as a gypsy fortuneteller. Except for the touch of melodrama in *A Comedy of Masks,* their failures are gray, not scarlet; of dullness, not excess. They bore rather than shock or outrage. No one should reproach Dowson for attempting a new form; a writer must explore many forms to learn in which he excels. Still, most readers will resent Dowson's novels, along with his translations, for the time they took from his poems. Brevity characterizes all of his best work, and the brief firefly of a single poem is far more precious than either of his elephantine novels.

CHAPTER 7

The Halo of Ghosts and Tears

THE AUTHOR of a study devoted to a minor poet is obligated to justify his choice. Is Dowson after all worth extended attention? A few modern critics, it is true, have questioned his status even as a minor figure. When Longaker's biography appeared in 1944, one reviewer charged that so slight a poet did not deserve so thorough a study, and another that the biographer had overpraised his subject. Six years later John Heath-Stubbs joined Dowson's detractors with *The Darkling Plain: A Study of the Later Fortunes of Romanticism in English Poetry from George Darley to W. B. Yeats*. Except for Yeats, he insisted, the English Decadents were men of small talent and performance. Oscar Wilde was a backwater; and of Johnson, Symons, and Dowson he wrote: "Dowson came nearest to success—but that is not very near. He survives, in a shadowy way, through the charm of, at most, two or three minor poems." [1] Such a view is neither rare nor surprising. Dowson was a traditionalist, and the twentieth century is an age which encourages experiment. He was clear, not ambiguous; emotional and often sentimental, not cerebral.

Heath-Stubbs, himself an excellent poet, is entitled to his preferences; but he errs when he says that Dowson "survives, in a shadowy way, through the charm of, at most, two or three minor poems." The survival of "Cynara" and "They Are Not Long" is anything but shadowy in Untermeyer and in countless other anthologies (as well as in the titles of books and motion pictures). What is more, they are often joined by "To One in Bedlam," "My Lady April," "A Last Word," "Extreme Unction," "You Would Have Understood Me," and others; moreover, Dowson's collected poems have recently been published in a new and definitive edition (1962). Admittedly Dowson is a poet whose directness and limited range do not lend themselves to ingenious interpretations, and whose pessimism will never attract as many readers as the romanticism of, for example, Mrs. Browning, a poet of similar range. Yet he is far more widely read today than in his own lifetime, when his three volumes of poetry—*Verses, The Pierrot of the Minute,* and *Decorations*—were printed in editions of approximately 330 copies each and then not exhausted until after his death. And he promises to be read as long as men admire precision and enjoy vicarious sighs.

A poet can endure in two ways: by influencing later poets or by delighting later readers. As an influence, Dowson cannot entirely be separated from the Decadence, which died as a movement with the nineteenth century but whose rich exoticism, illustrating the principle that art is its own excuse and does not need to make a point or preach a moral, survived into the next century and found expression in the work of the Imagists and of the early Wallace Stevens. As Wilde and Dowson reveled in catalogs of jewels and Huysmans in perfumes and flowers, so Stevens catalogs colors in "Sea Surface Full of Clouds," and Amy Lowell in "Lilacs" blends the decorous hues of New England with the barbarous beauties of the East:

> Lilacs,
> False blue,
> White,
> Purple,
> Color of lilac,
> You have forgotten your Eastern origin,
> The veiled women with eyes like panthers,
> The swollen, aggressive turbans of jeweled Pashas.[2]

In another aspect of the Decadence, its concern with decay, Dowson has more directly influenced a later poet. When he was graduating from Rugby at the age of eighteen, Rupert Brooke made a remarkable speech in which he described the English Decadents "as men who in the Garden of Life have built themselves rose bowers with careful hands, but, in the splendour of the sunset, sit pale and listless, because they

have seen the face of Death between the roses. . . ." Of Dowson
in particular he wrote that "he had created a new sigh." [3]
Brooke appropriated the sigh and also the sorrowful Alexan-
drines of "Cynara" for his own "Day That I Have Loved,"
"The Vision of the Archangels," and "Ante Aram." In a line
from "Ante Aram"—"And voice more sweet than the far plaint
of viols is"—he incorporates the melancholy "v" which Dowson
had called the most beautiful of letters; and the lovers in his
"Wayfarers," like those of Dowson in "Gray Nights," wander
the netherlands of death. But Brooke is probably the only
well-known poet who chose Dowson for his chief model. Never
an experimentalist, Dowson perfected old forms rather than
initiating new, and he has not been a major influence on later
poets. The general reader more than the practicing poet has
preserved his name.

What are the qualities which endear Dowson to that reader?
An artful brevity is the first hallmark of his writing. Except
for his two disastrous forays into the novel and his undistin-
guished translations, he wisely avoided the long and the mas-
sive. He lacked the power to sustain creation successfully in
the larger forms, but he worked in miniature with unfaltering
hands. His play runs a single act, not three or four; and his
best prose is less than a page. The forms he chose for his
poems are usually brief, not the epic or even the ballad, but
the sonnet and the villanelle, the rondeau and the shorter
rondel. Brevity is not without risks. A poet may economize to
the point of obscuring the sense and turn his poem into a
puzzle. But Dowson does not pose puzzles. His meaning is
evident without being obvious; he omits the superfluous but
not the essential. In a sense he is the Fabergé of poets. His
poems are like the nineteenth-century craftsman's Easter eggs
and pillboxes which, seemingly slight but hard with gold and
gems, open to reveal small treasures.

Littleness may extend to his content as well as his form. In
The Pierrot of the Minute we have seen the frequent smallness
of effect: the title, the repetition of "little," and the use of
butterflies to draw the Moon Maiden's car. Similarly in the
poems, he prefers the child to the adult and hails "Little lady
of my heart!" In "Villanelle of Sunset," not only is the heroine
a child, but she is further diminished into a white bird and a

tired flower to be worn on the poet's breast. Even when the subject is not normally small, even when it is adult love or death, he often reduces it to manageable dimensions by limiting the time and the scene along with the form: the time to a moment; the scene to a garden or a graveyard, a convent or a room in a madhouse.

In part, of course, such imposing of limits is necessary for all poets writing in the briefest of literary forms, the lyric. But in Dowson's case it is more than the exigencies of the lyric which compel him to brevity. Science baffled him; progress dismayed him; the largeness and loudness of industrialized England threatened to engulf him. Unable to retreat in distance, he retreated into his poems, into the little worlds which, because of his proportionate largeness, he could to a point control. In a world which since Dowson's day has grown more terrifying, where atom bombs have replaced cannons and where jet airliners whoosh through the sky and Greyhounds whirr along super highways, there is urgent need for microcosms which, far from dwarfing man, put him at ease by giving him something to grasp with his hands or to measure with his eyes, something to encompass and comprehend. The child, overshadowed by adults, takes refuge in dolls or toy soldiers; the adult, dwarfed by nature and machines, plants flowers in a pot or collects coins. This same urge Dowson satisfies in his writing. There is a need for moving vans but there is also a need for pillboxes; a need for epics but also for lyrics. With Dowson littleness is not pettiness; it is petiteness.

If brevity is the first hallmark of Dowson's writing, innocence is the second—the innocence of Adelaide and his worshipful love for her. Most of the Decadents were more concerned with sin than virtue. With Swinburne they sang both the "rapture and roses of vice" and the "lilies and languor of virtue," but they much preferred the roses. Dowson reversed the balance in his poems, if not in his life. His preference is clear in his treatment of the moon, a popular subject of the Decadents. Because she is fickle and inconstant, changing moods from night to night and expressions from minute to minute, now demurely secret behind a cloud, now exploding into gilt flamboyance, Baudelaire saw her as a divine courtesan. In "The Favours of the Moon," he imagines her addressing a child who lies asleep: " 'And you shall be loved by my lovers, courted by my courtiers. You shall be the queen of green-eyed men whose breasts I have also clasped in my nocturnal caresses; of those who love the sea, the vast tumultuous green sea, the formless and multiform water, the place where they are not, the woman whom they do not know, the sinister flowers that look like the censers of some unknown religion, the perfumes that disturb the will, and the wild and voluptuous beasts that are the emblems of their folly.' " [4] In Dowson, on the contrary, at least in his *Pierrot of the Minute,* the courtesan becomes a maiden. She descends to earth to teach a mortal the delights of love, but no lovers ever spent a more decorous evening. The goddess still shines but her glowing is that of Adelaide; she is white instead of gilt.

Dowson's brevity and innocence are irreproachable. His melancholy, however, is perhaps more open to criticism. There is no doubt that he is morbid, that he often wished to die and darkened his poems with the threat or presence of death. He can take a normally cheerful subject and infect it with his own black spirits. He can ask his sweetheart to help him seize the day and then make the day sound too dismal to be worth seizing. To read all of his poems at one sitting is to risk a surfeit of gloom. But taken in moderation they· are highly pleasurable; their grief is remote enough not to be shattering, close enough to summon vicarious tears. Catharsis is perhaps too strong a word for the process they work in us; Dowson was not writing Greek tragedy. As he intended, his people are pensive rather than passionate and tragic. His heroines are Cynara and Neobule, not Medea and Electra. There is still, however, a kind of cleansing. Because his subjects are smaller than life instead of larger, one feels protective toward them, proprietary, invited to share in their sadness without being overwhelmed.

If it is permissible to borrow a North American bird for a metaphor about an English poet, Dowson might be called the whippoorwill of literature. He is not a lark like Robert Herrick; he does not herald the morning or skim the afternoon. He flies at dusk or night. He is wistful and eerie, trailing into poignant silences. Modern criticism, remembering a time when the terms were overused, dislikes to speak of poets as singers and of poems as songs. But Yeats called "Villanelle of Sunset" "not speech, but perfect song," [5] and the same could be said of Dowson's other best poems. It is no mere poeticism, then, to compare him to a wistfully singing whippoorwill.

The birdlike delicacy of his art—its brevity, innocence, and sadness—is all the more remarkable in view of the fact that the Decadents were the beatniks of their day and that Dowson, in his personal habits, was as "beat" as the best (or worst) of them. After leaving Oxford without his degree, and increasingly after the suicide of his parents and the depletion of his funds, he frequented dives, inhabited rooms which today would be called "pads," and dressed with a casualness which bordered on slovenliness (though he did not grow a beard, he sometimes wore a mustache). The novelist Gertrude Atherton, who met him while visiting with friends at Pont-Aven, describes his appearance at the age of twenty-nine: "Aleece and I were sitting together when we saw Vachell crossing the square with a sad-looking object shambling beside him: a small man with nothing of youth in his bearing. He wore a black sweater, he was unshaven, his hair was long and dusty, his eyes were green, his lips looked like a smudge of red sealing wax, and he had no front teeth." [6] As Miss Atherton was soon to learn, he could clean himself up until he fitted the description by LeGallienne: "He was a frail appealing figure, with an almost painfully sensitive face, delicate as a silverpoint, recalling at once Shelley and Keats, too worn for one so young, haggard, one could not but surmise, with excessive ardours of too eager living." [7] But even LeGallienne hints at dissipation in the "too eager living." Certainly Dowson had a beatnik's contempt for the niceties of society, and his *Comedy of Masks* makes clear that he preferred Brodonowski's to a London drawing room. Like the novel, his poems intimate the beatnik life he lived, and his "wine and woman and song" are the identical pleasures with which the beatniks presumably console themselves for the meaninglessness of their universe.

But if Dowson was "beat" in appearance and actions and even in occasional allusions, his theory of art was staunchly Classical. The forms he used—the Petrarchan sonnet, the French villanelle, and others—demanded the highest discipline. Their pattern of rhymes and the length and number of their lines were rigidly fixed by tradition, and he did not deviate from his predecessors. In keeping with the forms, his treatment is orderly and exclusive; he selected his materials with care and omitted the rude and colloquial. Beatnik art in contrast is turbid and all-inclusive, lively instead of stately, with petulances and pungent colloquialisms, and a deliberate and successful attempt to shock. The most famous beatnik poem is called "Howl." It might also be called "Leer." But lively art is not always enduring. The morning paper is lively —until tomorrow. Had a beatnik written "Cynara," it is easy to imagine that the speaker would have cried for beer, not wine; that the lady of the bought red mouth would have been designated a "broad" or worse; and that the love affair would not have been left to the imagination. The title, of course, would have been changed to "Bessie" or "Gladys." Such photographic realism, mirroring a particular moment rather than glimpsing the ageless, would doubtless have proved an asset in Dowson's anemic novels; it is better to have a photograph than a blank film. But his poems have virtues more enduring than mere immediacy.

By living like a beatnik and yet by writing with Classical restraint Dowson, if anything, has increased the glamor of his legend. The great contrast between his disorderly life and his well-ordered art is intriguing. In the light of his life, the reserve of his poems becomes eloquent; one imagines that the poet has sinned and suffered magnificently but that he has had the good taste not to confess everything in print. Left to the reader's imagination, his sins and suffering assume titanic proportions, and he walks in a "halo of ghosts and tears." Long before he died, Dowson protested such an image of himself [8] and yet increased his halo by what he wrote and what he did not write.

With appropriateness, if not with originality, good minor poets are often said to represent the footpaths of literature. Dowson's path, it may be added, wanders through an antique garden where lilies nod languorously and rose petals redden the grass; where ivory-cheeked maidens weep beside quiet streams and wise children stare with the eyes of adults. The buoyant sun is a stranger to the place. Queen of the garden is the melancholy moon, and her beams are tears which silver the fallen petals. And yet her subjects do not resent her reign. For the zealous readers who ply them, the highways of Shakespeare and Milton are vital but a little terrifying in their crowded length and their hardness. With Dowson it is possible to meander at will through pleasant shadows with enough company for fellowship but not crowding. Literature has need of footpaths as well as highways.

Notes and References

Preface

1. Some critics have tried to demolish Dowson's aura of "ghosts and tears," his resemblance to a character out of Dumas Fils. The legend, no doubt, has exaggerated his dissipations and perhaps his bondage to Adelaide, but the fact remains that he did drink absinthe and did suffer unrequited love and that his own contemporaries—Harris, LeGallienne, Yeats, and others—recognized an air of doom about him.

2. Quoted by Mark Longaker, *Ernest Dowson* (Philadelphia, 1944), p. 265.

Chapter One

1. *The Savoy*, No. 2 (April, 1896), 66-67.

2. *Selected Works*, ed. by Richard Aldington (New York, 1948), p. 85.

3. *Baudelaire, Rimbaud, Verlaine: Selected Verse and Prose Poems*, ed. by Joseph M. Bernstein (New York, 1947), p. 169.

4. *The Savoy*, p. 192.

5. *The Autobiography* (New York, 1953), pp. 194-95.

6. "Love in Dreams," *Poems* (New York, 1914), II, 47.

7. An interesting discussion of Symons' indebtedness to "Cynara" appears in Longaker's *Ernest Dowson*, p. 84.

8. *Latin Poetry in Verse Translation*, ed. by L. R. Lind (Boston, 1957), p. 185.

9. Victor Plarr, *Ernest Dowson* (New York, 1914), p. 57, note 1.

Chapter Two

1. Quoted by Longaker, *Ernest Dowson*, pp. 77-78.

2. *The Poems of Ernest Dowson*, ed. by Arthur Symons (London, 1905), xv.

3. For the best treatment of Dowson and Adelaide, see Longaker's *Ernest Dowson*, pp. 73-79.

4. *Contemporary Portraits* (*Second Series*) (New York, 1919), p. 76.

5. *The Poems of Ernest Dowson,* ed. by Mark Longaker (Philadelphia, 1962), p. 80. Further quotations from *Poems* in this chapter will be identified by page references in the text.

6. *A Book of Airs* (Mount Vernon, undated), p. 6.

7. See Longaker's excellent discussion in *Ernest Dowson,* p. 27.

8. Plarr, *Ernest Dowson,* p. 79.

9. *Songs and Lyrics* (Mount Vernon, undated), p. 100.

10. Quoted by Mark Longaker in *The Stories of Ernest Dowson* (Philadelphia, 1947), p. 157.

11. Symons, *The Poems of Ernest Dowson,* xiv.

12. *Ibid.,* xxv.

13. *The Autobiography,* p. 197.

14. Plarr, *Ernest Dowson,* p. 57.

15. Arthur Symons, *Poems,* I, p. 118.

16. Quoted by Longaker, *Ernest Dowson,* p. 81.

17. *Latin Poetry in Verse Translation,* p. 102.

18. *The Poems* (Cambridge, 1952), p. 22.

19. *Ibid.,* p. 22.

20. "Ernest Dowson: An Interpretation," *The Catholic World,* C (November, 1914), 200.

21. *Contemporary Portraits,* p. 73.

22. The poem is dedicated to the novelist Conal O'Riordan, with whom Dowson toured Brittany and Flanders in 1895. Longaker suggests that the theme is betrayed friendship rather than divided love. When Dowson asked his friend to join him a second time in Brittany, in the fall of 1896, "O'Riordan found such a plan inconvenient. Dowson considered his friend's refusal a desertion. 'Exile' can be read in the light of these circumstances" (Longaker, *The Poems of Ernest Dowson,* p. 221).

23. Of Hélène, Longaker writes. "I have been unable to determine who Hélène was, although it is possible that she was another one of the poet's abstractions—an earlier and lesser Cynara" (*ibid.,* p. 233).

Chapter Three

1. Plarr, *Ernest Dowson,* p. 20.

2. *Ibid.,* pp. 83-84.

3. Quoted by Longaker, *Ernest Dowson,* p. 192.

4. *Against the Grain,* with an introduction by Havelock Ellis (New York, 1931), p. 104.

5. *The Poems of Ernest Dowson,* ed. by Mark Longaker, p. 40. Further quotations from *Poems* in this chapter will be identified by page references in the text.

6. Longaker, *Ernest Dowson,* p. 29.

7. *The Poetical Works of Christina Georgina Rossetti* (London, 1924), p. 417.

8. Quoted by Plarr, *Ernest Dowson,* p. 20.

9. Kallimachos, "Epitaph of Charidas of Kyrene," *Poems from the Greek Anthology,* trans. by Dudley Fitts (New York, 1956), p. 118.

10. Plarr, *Ernest Dowson,* p. 30.

11. Katherine Wheatley, "Ernest Dowson's 'Extreme Unction,'" *Modern Language Notes,* XXXVIII (May, 1923), 315.

Chapter Four

1. *A Literary History of England,* ed. by Albert C. Baugh (New York, 1948), p. 1484.

2. *The Men of the Nineties* (New York, 1921), pp. 60-61.

3. *The Poems of Ernest Dowson,* ed. by Mark Longaker, p. 153. Further quotations from *Poems* in this chapter will be identified by page references in the text.

4. *Modern American Poetry and Modern British Poetry,* ed. by Louis Untermeyer (New York, 1942), p. 334.

5. *The Works of Oscar Wilde* (New York, undated), XII, p. 162.

Chapter Five

1. Frank Harris, *Contemporary Portraits,* p. 67.

2. *The Stories of Ernest Dowson,* p. 12. Further quotations from *Stories* in this chapter will be identified by page references in the text.

3. *The Poems of Ernest Dowson,* ed. by Mark Longaker, p. 89.

4. Plarr, *Ernest Dowson,* p. 96.

5. *Contemporary Portraits,* p. 66.

Chapter Six

1. *The Men of the Nineties,* p. 58.

2. Plarr, *Ernest Dowson,* pp. 91-92.

3. Longaker, *Ernest Dowson,* pp. 124-25.

4. *A Comedy of Masks* (London, 1893) II, p. 113. Further quotations from *A Comedy* in this chapter will be identified by page references in the text.

5. *The House of Mirth* (New York, undated), p. 52.

6. *Epigrams,* illus. by Fritz Kredel (Mount Vernon, undated), p. 20.

7. *Ibid.,* p. 32.

8. Longaker, *Ernest Dowson,* p. 124.

9. *Adrian Rome* (New York, 1899), p. 42. Further quotations from *Adrian Rome* in this chapter will be identified by page references in the text.

Chapter Seven

1. (London, 1950), p. 150.

2. *A Shard of Silence,* ed. by G. R. Ruihley (New York, 1957), pp. 86-87.

3. *The Prose of Rupert Brooke,* ed. by Christopher Hassall (London, 1956), xv.

4. *Baudelaire, Rimbaud, Verlaine,* ed. by Joseph M. Bernstein, p. 149.

5. In his *Autobiography,* Yeats confesses a much less favorable opinion of Dowson himself: "I think Dowson's best verse immortal . . . but he was too vague and gentle for my affections. I understood him too well, for I had been like him but for the appetite that made me search out strong condiments" (187-88). In an earlier passage, however, he admits that Dowson also sought condiments of a sort: ". . . the last time I saw Dowson he was pouring out a glass of whiskey for himself in an empty corner of my room and murmuring over and over in what seemed an automatic apology, 'The first to-day' " (187).

6. *Adventures of a Novelist* (New York, 1932), p. 256.

7. *The Romantic '90's* (New York, 1926), p. 186.

8. Late in 1895, Dowson wrote to Sam Smith: "But I *do not* go about in Paris with a halo of ghosts and tears, having been gifted by God with a sense—common to you and myself but to how many other of our friends?—of humour! I occasionally smile, and even in Paris, at a late hour of the night, and Paris is later than London, have been known to laugh." Quoted by John Gawsworth in "The Dowson Legend," *Essays by Divers Hands,* ed. by E. H. W. Meyerstein (London, 1938), p. 119.

Selected Bibliography

PRIMARY SOURCES

1. Published in His Lifetime:

A Comedy of Masks. With Arthur Moore. London: William Heineman, 1893-94.
Dilemmas: Stories and Studies in Sentiment. London: Elkin Mathews, 1895.
Verses. London: Leonard Smithers, 1896.
The Pierrot of the Minute. London: Leonard Smithers, 1897.
Decorations: In Verse and Prose. London: Leonard Smithers, 1899.
Adrian Rome. With Arthur Moore. London: Methuen and Co. 1899.

2. Published after His Death:

The Poems of Ernest Dowson. Portland, Maine: Thomas B. Mosher, 1902.
The Poems of Ernest Dowson. Memoir by Arthur Symons. London: John Lane, The Bodley Head, 1905. Reprinted 1915, 1929.
Cynara: A Little Book of Verse. Portland, Maine: Thomas B. Mosher, 1907.
Poems and Prose. Memoir by Arthur Symons. New York: Boni and Liveright, 1919.
Complete Poems. New York: The Medusa Head, 1928.
The Pierrot of the Minute. San Francisco: The Windsor Press, 1932.
The Poems of Ernest Christopher Dowson. Ed. by Desmond Flower. London: Cassell and Co., 1934.
The Poems of Ernest Dowson. London: Unicorn Press, 1946.
Cynara: The Complete Lyrics of Ernest Dowson. Mount Vernon: The Peter Pauper Press, undated.
The Stories of Ernest Dowson. Ed. by Mark Longaker. London: W. H. Allen, 1947.
The Poems of Ernest Dowson. Ed. by Mark Longaker. Philadelphia: University of Pennsylvania Press, 1962.

3. Translations

Zola, Émile Edouard Charles Antoine. *La Terre*. London: Lutetian Society, 1894.

Couperus, Louis Marie Ann. *Majesty*. With Teixeira de Mattos. London: T. Fisher Unwin, 1894.

Muther, Richard. *The History of Modern Painting*. With G. A. Greene and A. C. Hillier. London: Henry and Co., 1896.

Balzac, Honoré de. *La Fille aux Yeux d'Or*. London: Leonard Smithers, 1896.

Choderlos de Laclos, Pierre Ambroise François. *Les Liaisons Dangereuses*. London: Privately printed, 1898.

Dubois, Guillaume. *Memoirs of Cardinal Dubois*. London: Leonard Smithers, 1899.

Voltaire, François Marie Arouet de. *La Pucelle d'Orleans*. London: Lutetian Society, 1899.

Goncourt, Edmond Louis Antoine de and Jules Alfred de Goncourt. *The Confidantes of a King: The Mistresses of Louis XV*. London: T. N. Foulis, 1907.

The Story of Beauty and the Beast. London: John Lane, 1908.

SECONDARY SOURCES

1. A Nutshell Library of Decadent Literature and Art

Bernstein, Joseph M., ed. *Baudelaire, Rimbaud, Verlaine: Selected Verse and Prose Poems*. New York: The Citadel Press, 1947. The best work, expertly translated by Arthur Symons and others, of three French Decadents, two of whom—Baudelaire and Verlaine—profoundly influenced Dowson.

The Book of the Rhymers' Club. London: Elkin Mathews, 1892; *The Second Book of the Rhymers' Club*. London: Elkin Mathews and John Lane, 1894. Anthologies containing the early work of Dowson, Yeats, Symons, Johnson, and their friends in the Rhymers' Club.

Huysmans, Joris Karl. *Against the Grain*. Introduction by Havelock Ellis. New York: Illustrated Editions Company, 1931. The Bible of the French Decadence, a plotless novel which excels in the description of bizarre sensations.

Pater, Walter. *The Renaissance: Studies in Art and Poetry*. Cleveland: The World Publishing Company (Meridian Books), 1961. The study which contains the famous aesthetic manifesto about the "hard, gemlike flame."

Selected Bibliography

The Savoy, No. 2 (April, 1896). A typical issue of the famous Decadent magazine, with drawings by Beardsley and a story and poem each by Dowson, Yeats, and Symons.

Von Holten, Ragnar. *L'Art Fantastique de Gustave Moreau*. Paris: Jean-Jacques Pauvert, 1960. A monograph, with reproductions in color and black and white, on the French painter who helped to inspire Wilde's *Salomé* and whose paintings are mentioned or described in *Against the Grain*, in *The Picture of Dorian Gray*, and in *A Comedy of Masks*.

Wilde, Oscar. *The Picture of Dorian Gray*. Introduction by Frances Winwar. New York: The World Publishing Co., 1946. The English equivalent to the French *Against the Grain*, as sensuous and far more exciting.

—————. *Salomé*. Illustrated by Aubrey Beardsley. London: Elkin Mathews and John Lane, 1894. The best Decadent play illustrated by the most famous Decadent artist.

2. Works about Dowson and His Times

Atherton, Gertrude. *Adventures of a Novelist*. New York: Blue Ribbon Books, Inc., 1932. Describes Miss Atherton's temporarily successful attempt to reform Dowson at Pont-Aven.

Bregy, Katherine. "Ernest Dowson: An Interpretation," *The Catholic World*, C (November, 1914), 193-205. A graceful article which frames Dowson in the Decadence but recognizes his uniqueness, particularly in his use of old French verse forms.

Brooke, Rupert. *The Prose*. Introduction by Christopher Hassall. London: Sidgwick and Jackson, 1956. Contains a lecture on modern poetry in which Brooke emphasizes the importance of Dowson and credits him with creating a "new sigh."

Flower, Newman. "Three Interesting Sinners," *Bookman*, LXIV (October, 1926), 148-50. Records a brief but haunting scene of Dowson in the grip of alcohol and inspiration.

Gawsworth, John. "The Dowson Legend," *Essays by Divers Hands*, New Series, Vol. XVII. Ed. by E. H. W. Meyerstein. London: Oxford University Press, 1938. An attempt to counteract the popular image of Dowson as a dissolute wastrel.

Harris, Frank. *Contemporary Portraits (Second Series)*. New York: Published by the author, 1919. Includes a colorful if sometimes inaccurate chapter on Dowson.

Heath-Stubbs, John. *The Darkling Plain: A Study of the Later Fortunes of Romanticism in English Poetry from George Darley to W. B. Yeats*. London: Eyre and Spottiswoode, 1950.

An articulate if biased expression of the viewpoint that Dowson and the other English Decadents, except for Yeats, are not merely minor but negligible.

Jackson, Holbrook. *The Eighteen Nineties.* New York: Mitchell Kennerley, 1913. Though half a century old, the best general study of the decade. Illustrations by Beardsley, Beerbohm, and other artists of the period.

Jennings, Richard. "Books in General," *New Statesman and Nation,* XXIX (March 31, 1945), 210. A review of Mark Longaker's biography and a chance for the author to include some thoughts of his own on Dowson: for example, that the poet owed a debt to Christina Rossetti as well as to Swinburne.

LeGallienne, Richard. *The Romantic '90's.* Garden City, New York: Doubleday, Page and Co., 1926. A luminous reminiscence by a onetime Decadent; contains affectionate memoirs of Dowson, Johnson, Wilde, and others.

Longaker, Mark. *Ernest Dowson.* Philadelphia: University of Pennsylvania Press, 1944. The definitive biography of Dowson, sensitive, thorough, reliable.

Muddiman, Bernard. *The Men of the Nineties.* New York: G. P. Putnam's Sons, 1921. A lively account of the writers, publishers, and publications of the 1890's.

Percival, M. O. and C. E. Andrews, eds. *Poetry of the Nineties.* New York: Harcourt, Brace & Co., 1926. A period anthology with a discrimniating introduction and a generous if uneven selection of Dowson's poems.

Plarr, Victor. *Ernest Dowson.* New York: Laurence J. Gomme. 1914. A poor biography, rambling and evasive, with painful attempts at humor and a patronizing attitude toward the subject ("poor Ernest Dowson"). Valuable, however, for its bibliography of Dowson's publications during his lifetime and for the inclusion of previously unpublished letters which he wrote to Plarr.

Rhys, Ernest *Everyman Remembers.* New York: Cosmopolitan Book Corporation, 1931. Readable reminiscences of Dowson and others of his period, by one of the founders of the Rhymers' Club.

Sherard, Robert Harborough. *Twenty Years in Paris.* Philadelphia: George W. Jacobs and Co., 1905. Contains an account of Dowson in Paris, and also during his last days in London, where Sherard looked after him until he died.

Symons, Arthur. "Mr. Ernest Dowson," *Athenaeum,* I (March 3,

Selected Bibliography

1900), 274. An affectionate obituary which summarizes Dowson's career and predicts the permanence of his best poems.

————. *The Symbolist Movement in Literature.* New York: E. P. Dutton and Co., Inc., 1958. The classic study of Verlaine, Rimbaud, Huysman, and other French Decadents.

Thomas, W. R. "Ernest Dowson at Oxford," *Nineteenth Century,* CIII (April, 1928), 560-66. An article which helped to dispel the myths, encouraged by Symons, that Dowson lacked intellect and that he became addicted to hashish at Oxford.

Untermeyer, Louis, ed. *Modern American Poetry and Modern British Poetry* (Combined New and Enlarged Edition). New York: Harcourt, Brace & World, Inc., 1962. Contains an excellent short summary of Dowson's achievement and a small but well-chosen sampling of his work.

Wheatley, Katherine. "Ernest Dowson's 'Extreme Unction,'" *Modern Language Notes,* XXXVIII (May, 1923), 315. Points out Dowson's indebtedness to *Madame Bovary* for the imagery of "Extreme Unction."

Winwar, Frances. *Oscar Wilde and the Yellow Nineties.* New York: Harper and Brothers, 1958. An eloquent study of Wilde and his period, with several pages devoted to Dowson.

Yeats, William Butler. *The Autobiography.* New York: The Macmillan Company, 1953. In the section called "The Trembling of the Veil," an unkind look at Dowson the man, a kinder look at his poems.

Index

Aestheticism, 17-19

Atherton, Gertrude, 106

Balzac, Honore de, 87

Bantock, Granville, 73

Baudelaire, Pierre Charles, 18-19, 21-22, 27, 42, 47, 83, 104

Beardsley, Aubrey, 19-20, 23-25, 27, 75

Beerbohm, Max, 24

Bentley, (Publisher), 91

Bookman, 91

Bregy, Katherine, 51-52

Brooke, Rupert, 102, 103

Browning, Elizabeth Barrett, 46, 100, 101

Browning, Robert, 46, 65, 100

Campion, Thomas, 34

Carew, Thomas, 49

Catullus, 31

The Century Guild Hobby Horse, 45

Coleridge, Samuel Taylor, 18

Collins, Wilkie, 96

Darley, George, 101

Decadence, *see* Decadents

Decadents, 17, 19, 20-31, 45-47, 57, 60, 61, 64, 70, 71, 78, 79, 81, 100-102, 106

DeQuincey, Thomas, 18, 27, 81

Dickens, Charles, 96

Dobson, Austin, 51, 70

Dowson, Ernest,

  As Decadent, 17, 20, 22-31, 45-47, 71, 102, 106;

Contributor to *The Savoy;* 25, 26, *The Yellow Book,* 24, 26; Conversion to Catholicism, 29, 30;

Friends and influences: Ancient Roman writers, 31, 45, 47-49, 65, 70; Beardsley, 27; Cavalier poets, 49, 50, 51; Cult of childhood and little girls, 36-40, 83, 95; Adelaide Foltino-wicz, 32-34, 37, 40-42, 44, 46, 48, 56, 58, 77, 81, 83, 95, 104, 105; Nature, 57-61; Religion, 65-69, 84; Swinburne, 27, 28, 53, 58; Verlaine, 30, 31, 54; Wilde, 27;

Personal appearance, 106, 107;

Themes: Death, 35-39, 49-54, 61-65, 72, 82, 95, 105; Love, 32-35, 37, 44, 52, 54;

Summary and appraisal, 101-8

Works:

Collections:

Decorations, 30, 32, 80, 102

Dilemmas, 24

Verses, 32, 102

Novels:

Adrian Rome, 86, 90, 91, 96-100; *Marian Brabant,* 98; *Gerald Brooke,* 100; *Syvia Drew,* 97-99; *Miss Lancaster,* 99; *Mrs. Vesper,* 98, 99

A Comedy of Masks, 20, 28, 37, 90-97, 99, 100, 105; *Eve,* 92, 94; *Lady Garnett,* 92, 93, 99; *Kitty,* 92, 95, 97; *Lightmark,* 92, 95, 97; *Mary,* 92; *Oswyn,* 92, 94, 95, 97; *Philip Rain-ham,* 92-95, 97

Index

Index

Index